ROYAL WEDDING
The Souvenir Album

Alison James

Danann
BOOKS

Danann BOOKS

First Published Danann Publishing Ltd 2018

CAT NO: DAN0377

Photography courtesy of

Getty images:

J. A. Hampton / Stringer	Max Mumby/Indigo	Kirsty Wigglesworth
Fox Photos / Stringer	Anwar Hussein	Oli Scarff
Topical Press Agency / Stringer	Princess Diana Archive / Stringer	Paul Gilham
Print Collector	Hulton Deutsch	Julian Finney
Popperfoto	Pool/Tim Graham Picture Library	Underwood Archives
Hulton Archive / Stringer	David Levenson	Fred Ramage
Michael Ward	Derek Hudson	Paul Popper/Popperfoto
Rolls Press/Popperfoto	Bob Thomas/Popperfoto	Paul A. Hebert / Stringer
Bettmann	Sahm Doherty	Chris Jackson
Keystone / Stringer	Ben Stansall	Daniel Leal-Olivas
Hulton Royals Collection	Brooks Kraft	Steve Back
Tim Graham Photo Library	Wpa Pool	David M. Benett
Stf / Staff	Odd Andersen	Uk Press Pool

Book layout & design Darren Grice at Ctrl-d

Copy Editor Tom O'Neill

Made in EU.

ISBN: 978-1-912332-13-7

Contents

A Princely Marriage is the brilliant edition of a universal fact, and as such rivets mankind'

Introduction

The aim of every wedding is to be a joyful and memorable occasion for all concerned but there is, as Bagehot famously said, little more riveting — not to mention thrilling, exciting and spectacular — than a Royal Wedding. And a British Royal Wedding at that. *'No one does pageantry quite like the British,'* one American spectator at the Duke and Duchess of Cambridge's wedding in April 2011 was so rightly heard to observe. While, in 1948, legendary playwright Noel Coward wrote after the nuptials of the then Princess Elizabeth and Duke of Edinburgh that the wedding was, *'English tradition at its best'.*

As we celebrate the wedding of Prince Harry to US actress Miss Meghan Markle — and also that of Princess Eugenie of York to wine merchant, Mr Jack Brooksbank — what better time to look back at some of the most memorable Royal marriage ceremonies in recent times?

It is only in the last 200 years or so that our Royal Weddings have become national, and more recently international, events to be celebrated with the people rather than private family affairs conducted and contained within the inner sanctums of Royal palaces and castles.

It was in celebration of the wedding between Princess Charlotte of Wales, the only daughter of King George IV, and Leopold of Saxe-Coburg, in May 1816, that souvenirs celebrating a Royal marriage became available for the first time. Huge crowds lined the Mall in London to cheer the Princess and her new husband, although they were married in the Crimson Drawing Room at Carlton House, the home of the bride's father who was then Prince Regent. Tragically the young Princess died in childbirth in November 1817, having given birth to a stillborn son.

The wedding of Charlotte's cousin, Queen Victoria, to Prince Albert on February 10 1840 took place in the Chapel Royal of St James' Palace. The first wedding of a reigning Queen of England for 300 years, it was at this marriage ceremony of the young bride and her German consort that many wedding traditions, both Royal and non-Royal, came into being.

Before Victoria, brides did not, as a rule, wear white. It was more traditional to wear colours — red, blue and even black were popular choices, with gold or silver embroidery running through the gowns of well-to-do brides. Victoria chose to wear white for several reasons. She stated that on her wedding day she would be making her vows as Albert's future wife, not as the monarch and, therefore, wearing the simple purity of white was more fitting. She chose a white silk dress, made from silk spun at Spitalfields, in London, and Honiton lace, which was worked at the village of Beer in Devon — thus boosting both Britain's silk and lace trades. Victoria also wished to be visible as possible to the crowds that thronged the processional route from Buckingham Palace to St James' and this would surely be more possible if she wore a dress that stood out rather than merged into the background. She was delighted with the crowd's reaction. *'They cheered us really most warmly and heartily — the crowd was immense,'* she wrote.

In a further first, this Royal trendsetter begat a new fashion by having 12 bridesmaids to carry her 18-foot-long train. Victoria unwittingly started another Royal Wedding tradition when she decreed that a sprig of myrtle (known as the herb of everlasting love) from her wedding bouquet should be planted at her favourite retreat, Osborne House, on the Isle of Wight. From that small sprig grew a bush that has supplied cuttings for the bouquets of Royal brides ever since. It is also with thanks to Victoria that Royal newly-weds married in London appear on the Buckingham Palace balcony. After her daughter Vicky's wedding to the Prussian Crown Prince in the chapel at St James in November 1858, the Queen felt sorry for the crowds who had been unable to catch a glimpse of the bride and groom, and so she ordered Vicky and Fritz, along with other members of the Royal Family, out onto the balcony.

As technology has advanced, Royal Weddings have become more accessible to the public. The first regal wedding to be properly captured by photography was that between Victoria and Albert's eldest son, Albert Edward, to Alexandra of Denmark in March 1863, and many images were taken of the bride and groom, bridesmaids, page boys and wedding cakes. The wedding of our present Queen's parents, George VI and Queen Elizabeth, in April 1923, was the first to be filmed. Their younger daughter, Margaret's, wedding to Antony Armstrong Jones in May 1960 was the first to be televised to a national and international audience. While it's claimed an estimated two billion people worldwide witnessed the wedding between Prince William and Catherine Middleton in April 2011. Thanks to social media, the wedding of Harry and Meghan will arguably be seen by more people than any other Royal Wedding.

But wonderful though the Smart phone, Ipad and tablet are, nothing compares to the joy of browsing through a beautiful album of beloved and cherished wedding photos. We hope you enjoy our very special Royal Souvenir one...

Above:
William, Duke of Cambridge and Catherine, Duchess of Cambridge leave Buckingham Palace after their Wedding reception in Prince Charles' vintage Aston Martin DB6 Volante, April 29 2011, London

'It was my duty to marry Bertie and I fell in love with him afterwards'

Bertie & Elizabeth

APRIL 26 1923

The morning of April 26th 1923 dawned grey, gloomy and wet — hardly ideal wedding day weather — but this did nothing to dampen the thousands of well-wishers lining the streets of London waiting to celebrate the marriage between His Royal Highness, the Prince Albert of Great Britain, and the Lady Elizabeth Bowes Lyons.

This wedding between the second son of King George V and Queen Mary, and the youngest daughter of the Earl and Countess of Strathmore would prove to be ground-breaking in several, highly significant ways. To begin with, for the first time in five centuries the son of a reigning monarch was marrying in Westminster Abbey — the thousand-year-old former Cathedral which in 1560 had become what is known as a Church of England *'Royal Peculiar'*. Princess Mary, the sister of Prince Albert, or Bertie as he was known, had married there in 1922. The day was such a success with both the monarchy and the country as a whole, that it was the obvious choice for the next Royal Wedding. Prior to this, Royal marriages had taken place in smaller, more private venues such as the Chapel Royal at St James Palace or St George's Chapel, Windsor Castle.

In another *'first'*, cinema films were to be made of the ceremony — although the idea to broadcast the service on the radio had been vetoed by church leaders as it was feared people *'might hear the service, perhaps even some of them sitting in public houses, with their hats on!'*. In the event, by 9pm on April 26th, Gaumont Cinemas announced that they had produced 25 million feet of film which were available to view that very evening.

Lastly there was the question of the bride herself. Although a descendent of Scottish King, Robert the Bruce, and the daughter of an Earl, Elizabeth was a *'commoner'*. Just 10 years earlier, a non-royal marrying a Prince or Princess of the blood Royal would have been unthinkable. However, World War One had seen off many European Royal dynasties and therefore the British aristocracy became the breeding ground to source a royal spouse.

A *'commoner'* 22-year-old Elizabeth may have been but Bertie, 27 and known as Bertie, had to work extremely hard to woo her. Originally meeting as children in 1905, the pair became reacquainted at a dance in 1920. From the off, the shyly diffident Bertie was smitten with flirtatious, gregarious and oh-so-pretty Elizabeth — but it was not exactly mutual. She was fond enough of her high-born suitor but nevertheless turned down two marriage proposals — it was whispered this was because she was in love with someone else, possibly even his elder brother the Prince of Wales, although the official line was that she did not wish to commit to the demands of royal life. However, after Elizabeth had been a bridesmaid for Princess Mary in 1922, she deigned to accept Bertie's third proposal of marriage and in doing so a large sapphire and diamond engagement ring in a platinum setting was slid onto the third finger of her left hand.

On January 14th 1923, the day before the engagement was officially announced, King George V wrote in his diary *'Bertie informed us that he was engaged to Elizabeth Bowes Lyon, to which we gladly gave our consent. I trust they will be very happy'*.

THE ROYAL WEDDING

ALL HAPPINESS ATTEND THEM.

During the three-month engagement, Elizabeth, like Meghan Markle was to do 95 years later, became acquainted with Royal life — although unlike Meghan, Elizabeth stayed chastely under her parents' roof while her Prince continued to live at Buckingham Palace. A photographic portrait of the happy couple was released just three days after the engagement was announced, while individual portraits were also drawn by the American artist John Singer Sargent.

Elizabeth was seen as a breath of fresh Scottish air, immediately endearing herself to the British public by giving two interviews to the press — something which had never happened before. Her mother-in-law to be, Queen Mary, was not impressed but chose to blame the newspapers rather than Elizabeth. *'How tiresome the newspaper people have been interviewing E, such a shame,'* reads an entry in her diary. Before they married, Bertie and Elizabeth made one very important visit to the Edinburgh headquarters of McVitie and Price, the bakers who had been commissioned to make the principal Royal Wedding cake.

This would turn out to be a nine-feet tall, many tiered fruit cake — an elaborately decorated, architectural masterpiece hewn from royal icing.

As April 26 approached, wedding presents began to arrive. Elizabeth received two tiaras — a diamond diadem in the shape of a garland of wild roses from her father while her future father-in-law, George V, gifted her a diamond and turquoise tiara in addition to other jewellery pieces fashioned from the same gemstones. Queen Mary presented her soon-

Above:
A vintage postcard celebrating the Royal Wedding of Prince Albert Duke of York, to Elizabeth Bowes-Lyon

Right:
HRH Princess Elizabeth and Philip Mountbatten, Duke of Edinburgh, on the occasion of their engagement at Buckingham Palace in London

to-be daughter-in-law with a diamond and sapphire necklace while the Prince of Wales, Bertie's elder brother, gave Elizabeth a fur stole. The groom meanwhile received a 17th century clock from his royal relatives, a car from his big brother, and a miniature painting of Elizabeth set in a jewelled frame from his mother-in-law to be. Joint gifts included a set of enamelled spoons with strainers from the King and Queen of Norway who also happened to be Bertie's uncle and aunt, an Ostrich-feather mantlet from South African Ostrich farmers, and one thousand golden-eyed needles from the worshipful company of needle-makers!

As with every wedding, there was much anticipation and excitement about the bride's dress. This turned out to be anything but traditional. Fashioned by court dressmaker Madame Handley Seymour, it was a 1920s vision of a medieval-styled gown and was made from chiffon moire which had been dyed to match the ivory shade of the *'Pointe de Flanders'* lace veil lent by Queen Mary. Embellished with panels of silver lame, gold embroidery and pearl and paste beads, the gown featured not one but two trains — one falling from the shoulders, the other from the hips — both made from tulle and, at the bride's request, Nottingham lace. Elizabeth chose not to wear either of her new tiaras to hold her veil in place, choosing instead to secure it with a wreath of myrtle leaves, white roses and white heather. On her feet, she wore shoes of ivory silk moire embroidered with silver roses and she carried a bouquet of roses, lily-of-the-valley, and a sprig of myrtle. Although the dress was described by the Times newspaper as *'the simplest ever made for a Royal Wedding'*, Elizabeth was clearly very happy with it. *'Up by 10. Put on my wedding dress aided by Suzanne and Catherine. It looked lovely'* she wrote in her diary on the morning of the wedding,

Being a Royal Wedding, timings were of the upmost importance. *'The actual service begins at Westminster Abbey at half past eleven o'clock today,'* newspapers reported on the morning of April 26. *'Members of the Royal family will arrive at five minutes past 11 o'clock. The bridegroom will arrive at the West door at 25 minutes past 11 o'clock. The bride, accompanied by the Earl of Strathmore, arrives at the Abbey at 28 minutes past 11 o'clock'.*

While the groom, dressed in the uniform of a group captain of the Royal Air Force, and his elder brother, the Prince of Wales, departed Buckingham Palace by carriage, his bride was preparing to leave her

parents' London home — 17 Bruton Street — for the last time as a single woman and commoner. Photographs show her stepping out onto the pavement, her dress covered by a cape of ermine, and a curious half-smile on her face. Lady Elizabeth and her father drove the short distance to Westminster Abbey by State Landau coach, escorted by four mounted police officers. As the crowds cheered, Elizabeth smiled broadly and waved, later commenting that she was deeply touched by the affection shown by well-wishers. As the coach pulled up outside the Abbey, the clouds miraculously parted. *'The sun actually began to shine as Elizabeth entered the Abbey,'* Bertie later wrote in his diary.

Accompanied by her eight bridesmaids — all dressed in simple white gowns of crepe de chine — Elizabeth and the Earl of Strathmore started

as if to make their way down the aisle. But then fate took a hand. There was a delay in the wedding procession as a member of the clergy fainted. In a spontaneous gesture, Elizabeth took the opportunity to place her bouquet on the tomb of the Unknown Soldier in remembrance of all those who had lost their lives fighting for their country. This had extra resonance for her as one of her brothers had been killed in World War One. Elizabeth's action captured the imagination of the nation, setting a precedent for Royal brides ever since.

To the strains of *'Lead Us Heavenly Father Lead Us'*, the bridal party finally made their way up the aisle, witnessed by almost 2000 guests. Waiting for Elizabeth was Bertie whose eyes, the Times noted *'were shining with a look of happiness'* and continued by commenting that bride and groom *'seemed to think of no one but each other'*. As tradition dictated, Elizabeth promised to obey her royal husband. The Archbishop of Canterbury, Randall Davidson, conducted the service while the Archbishop of York, Cosmo Lang, gave the address, advising the couple to resolve to live *'a noble married life now their separate lives had been made one'*. Having signed the marriage register in the Chapel of Edward the Confessor, the new Duke and Duchess of York as they were now to be known, left the Abbey and travelled back to Buckingham Palace in the Glass Coach. Over a million, cheering people lined the route and as many as possible swarmed down the Mall towards the Palace once the wedding party had arrived back, demanding to see Elizabeth and Bertie. At 1.15pm with the King and Queen accompanying them, the beaming newly-weds stepped out on the Buckingham Palace balcony — smiling and waving to the vast crowds below.

A wedding breakfast for just 60 guests in the state dining room —

decorated with pink tulips and white lilac — followed. On the menu were such delights as *'Consomme a la Windsor'*, *'Cotelettes d'Agneau Prince Albert'*, and *'Fraiches Duchesse Elizabeth'*. Then it was time for the Duchess to change into her going away outfit — a grey two piece and brown cloche hat — and for the couple to leave on honeymoon. Their friends and family showering them with rose petals, they climbed into an open Laudau carriage which would take them to Waterloo Station where they would catch a special train to Polesdon Lacey in Surrey for the first leg of their honeymoon. The next day Bertie wrote to his mother, expressing his joy and happiness at being married — *'I am very, very happy now with my little darling'*. Elizabeth, however, seems to have been missing her family dreadfully. *'I could not say anything to you about how utterly miserable I was at leaving you and Father and David (her brother). I could not ever have said it to you but you know I love you more than anyone in the world, mother, and you do know it, don't you?'* Considering Elizabeth then contracted whooping cough on the second part of the honeymoon at Glamis Castle in Scotland, perhaps the trip wasn't the greatest success, causing Bertie to write, again to his mother, that it was *'so unromantic to catch whooping cough on your honeymoon'*.

However, if the honeymoon failed to live up to expectations, the same cannot be said for the marriage as a whole. *'Elizabeth will be a splendid partner in your work and share with you and help you in all you have to do,'* wrote King George V to his son shortly after the marriage. This proved to be true as Elizabeth supported Bertie, or George VI as he became, when he was forced, in December 1936, to take the throne following the abdication of his brother, Edward VIII. Elizabeth gave him the confidence and belief to rule, in addition to making a happy, harmonious home for him and their two daughters, the Princesses Elizabeth and Margaret Rose. When Bertie died in February 1952, leaving Elizabeth a widow at just 51, she felt as if she'd lost her soul mate. *'He was my whole life,'* she wrote on the day he died.

'One can only be deeply thankful for the utterly happy years we had together.'

David & Wallis

In complete contrast to the joy of Bertie and Elizabeth's Big Day, the wedding of his elder brother, the former King Edward VIII (known as David), and the twice divorced, Wallis Simpson, was a very subdued affair. Having virtually been banished from Britain, the couple were married at Château de Candé, a castle outside the French city of Tours, on June 3 1937, with fewer than 20 guests in attendance. The wedding was on what would have been King George V's 72nd birthday and Queen Mary was convinced the wedding had been scheduled for then as a deliberate slight. No member of David's family attended.

Wallis Simpson was dressed in *'soft blue crepe with a tight, buttoned bodice, a halo-shaped hat of the same colour, shoes and gloves to match. At her throat was a tremendous diamond-&-sapphire brooch. She carried a prayer book, had no bouquet but wore a large lavender orchid at her waist.'* She walked down the aisle to the march from Handel's *'Judas Maccabeus'*. The groom wore morning dress and seemed very nervous. According to reports, his hands shook terribly when he placed the ring, of traditional Welsh gold, on his bride's finger and shrieked *'I will'* in a high-pitched voice as he said his vows.

After the ceremony, there was champagne, salad and a few speeches before the Duke and Duchess of Windsor, as they would now be known, climbed into their limousine, driven by George Ladbrooke, the Duke's chauffeur of 17 years, and sped away from the chateau. Ahead of them went 226 pieces of luggage, including 183 trunks. For their honeymoon, they travelled to Austria on the Orient Express.

The wedding itself hadn't been promising but the marriage lasted 35 years, only ending when the Duke passed away in 1972.

Left:
The Duke and Duchess of Windsor gaze from a balcony on their wedding day

'The Wedding was the first ray of sunshine during that austere period after the war'

Elizabeth & Philip

NOVEMBER 20 1947

London 1947 and the UK capital was still bruised, battered and bomb-scarred following World War Two which had ended two years before. Something was needed to help lift the gloom of those long years of austerity, rationing and hardship. Something that looked forward rather than back, and brought a sense of hope, colour and excitement the whole nation could rejoice in. What better, then, than the wedding of a beautiful young Princess, the heir to the British throne, and a handsome Viking-like Prince who were truly, madly, deeply — and genuinely — in love? In a happy twist of fate that is just what happened on November 20 1947 when the Princess Elizabeth married Lieutenant Philip Mountbatten, former Prince of Greece. However, the path to true love — and eventually Westminster Abbey — didn't exactly run smoothly.

Both great, great grandchildren of Queen Victoria, the couple first met as teenagers just before the outbreak of war in 1939. Thirteen-year-old Elizabeth, known in the family as Lilibet, developed an instant teenage crush on the 18-year-old tall, blond and handsome midshipman who had been instructed to keep her and her younger sister, Margaret Rose, entertained while their parents, King George VI and Queen Elizabeth, were touring the Royal Naval College, Dartmouth. During the war years, Lilibet and Philip met occasionally whenever Philip's leave allowed. They corresponded as friends and the young princess kept a framed photo of Philip by her bed. When the war ended in May 1945, Lilibet, now 19, was hopeful their friendship would turn into something more.

Over that summer, the two met whenever possible and started to fall in love. Not that they rushed into anything. Philip was on his ship in the Far East for much of the next year, leaving Lilibet to burgeoning royal duties. But on August 11 1946, while at Balmoral Castle in the Scottish Highlands, 25-year-old Philip asked Lilibet to marry him. She accepted immediately, even though her very protective father had not given them his permission. It was a secret engagement but word soon got out. Lilibet was summoned by her unhappy parents who were worried about their young daughter marrying so worldly a man as Philip. But Lilibet was quietly determined to be with the man she had loved since she was just 13 and would not give in. She stood up to her father saying that as her life would be one of duty to her country, surely she should be allowed to marry the man she loved. *'After all you married Mummy,'* Elizabeth argued. *'She wasn't even Royalty — Philip is.'* Finally, a compromise was reached. The King grudgingly agreed to consent to the engagement but it must remain secret while he, the Queen and the Princesses toured South Africa for three months during the Spring of 1947. Lilibet had no choice but to comply.

Once back in London and reunited, Lilibet and Philip set about making plans. Having turned 21, the Princess was now officially an adult and unwilling to wait any longer. On July 10 1947 — almost a year after Lilibet had accepted Philip's clandestine proposal, the following announcement was made. *'It is with the greatest pleasure that the King and Queen announce the betrothal of their dearly beloved daughter the Princess Elizabeth to Lieutenant Philip Mountbatten RN . . . to which union the*

King has gladly given his consent.' Elizabeth's dresser and former nanny, Margaret *'Bobo'* MacDonald, announced, *'We got engaged!'* talking, as she often did, as if she and the Princess were one and the same. The news was immediately welcomed in other quarters with former Prime Minister Winston Churchill commenting that it was *'a flash of colour on the hard road we have to travel.'* Within days, official engagement photographs of the happy couple had been released of a proud looking Philip in his naval

uniform and a radiantly beaming Lilibet, sporting a diamond engagement ring designed by her husband-to-be and made from stones given to him by his mother from the tiara she had worn on her own wedding day. A similar gesture was to be repeated over 70 years on when Philip's grandson, Prince Harry, became engaged to Meghan Markle and presented her with a ring of his own design, made up of diamonds that had belonged to his late mother Diana, Princess of Wales.

As Royal Weddings go, Lilibet and Philip's was not a grand affair. The country was in dire straits and in the circumstances, the King felt Lilibet and Philip should have a relatively quiet, relatively small service and suggested St George's Chapel, Windsor as the venue. The Queen and Lilibet, however, wanted a big wedding in Westminster Abbey. They got their wish but it was scaled back, nevertheless. Due to shortages of timber for housebuilding, no spectator stands were erected along the route from Buckingham Palace to the Abbey and few decorations were in evidence. The King had wanted Lilibet and Philip to wait until the next summer to tie the knot, the bride was adamant it should take place that November.

Although the couple received the usual jewels, china and ornamental glassware from family and friends, the 3000 wedding presents they received from the public makes for the most interesting reading — the King having relaxed the rule that the couple should only receive gifts from those known to them in order to make the people feel part of the proceedings. Tea cosies, lace, and countless pairs of nylon stockings, which were still on ration, arrived at St James' Palace. The people of Leamington Spa sent a washing machine while the Women's Voluntary Service gifted a refrigerator. Two women sent a Siamese kitten while a turkey arrived from America because the giver believed there was nothing to eat in Great Britain.

As regards to the wedding gown, Lilibet needed to tread carefully as

Left & Right:
H R H Princess Elizabeth and Philip Mountbatten, Duke of Edinburgh, on the occasion of their engagement at Buckingham Palace in London

rationing was still in force, although she was granted 200 hundred extra clothing coupons for her bridal ensemble plus an extra 23 for each of her eight bridesmaids. Hundreds of clothing coupons were also sent in by members of the public but these had to be returned as it was illegal to transfer use. Couturier Norman Hartnell, who had been making clothes for Queen Elizabeth and the Princesses since the mid 1930s, was chosen to design the wedding dress after submitting preliminary sketches. Looking for inspiration, Hartnell visited a London art gallery where he came across a painting — *'Primavera'* by the Italian artist Botticelli. The figures in the painting with their trailing garlands of blossoms had been inspired by Flora, the classical goddess of flowers, and the coming of Spring. To the designer the image suggested the promise of growth, new beginnings and new life - just what was required after the bleak war years. In the event, the dress took 3000 clothing coupons and cost £1200 — worth over £300,000 in today's money — but. . . it was a masterpiece. The satin gown shimmered and sparkled with stars embroidered in crystals and 10,000 costume pearls which had been sourced in the USA. The 15 feet train was decorated with white roses worked in padded satin and sheeves of corn in diamante and pearl embroidery. The creation was such a closely guarded secret that Hartnell had the windows of his workroom whitewashed. Princess Elizabeth's outfit was completed with ivory duchesse satin high-heeled sandals, trimmed with silver and seed pearl buckles, made by Edward Rayne. The House of Hartnell also created the bridesmaid's dresses — from ivory silk tulle with a tightly fitted bodice. The two small pageboys — Prince Michael of Kent and Prince William of Gloucester, Lilibet's cousins - wore Royal Stuart tartan kilts with frilled white shirts and lace jabots.

The morning of November 20 was damp, cold and grey. Lilibet reportedly said little as Hartnell, his assistants and her own ladies dressed her. But there were to be a few hiccups. The *'Sunray'* tiara, the *'something borrowed'* from her mother and formed from diamonds that had originally been gifted to Queen Mary from Queen Victoria on her wedding day in 1893, snapped in two as it was placed on her head. Her mother tried to calm her, saying, *'Don't worry my dear — there is time and more than one tiara in this palace.'* But Lilibet was intent on wearing that particular diadem. It was taken, by police escort, to the Royal Jewellers, Garrard, where it was hastily repaired. The tiara was then rushed back to the

Palace for the Princess to wear — the repair just visible as a slight gap between the central fringe and the spike to its right. To add to the panic, the bride had been unable to find the two pearl necklaces she had planned to wear. Both pieces had huge historical significance with the shorter one thought to have belonged to Queen Anne, the last Stuart Queen. The second necklace is said to have belonged to Queen Caroline, the consort of King George II. Both pieces had been left to

the Crown by Queen Victoria and given to Elizabeth as a wedding present by her father. After a frantic search, the pearls were finally located alongside the wedding presents at St James Palace, having mistakenly been put on display. Finally, Lilibet's bouquet of white orchids — complete with sprig of myrtle as royal tradition dictated — had also gone AWOL. With only minutes to go, the flowers were eventually located in the porter's lodge ice-box where a footman had placed them to keep them fresh.

Despite these dramas, Lilibet made it to the Abbey on time for the wedding, due to start at 11.30am. She and her father rode from the Palace to the Abbey in the Glass Coach. *'The crowds were enormous,'* one magazine reported. *'And it was a happy, good-tempered crowd obviously determined to enjoy its brief escape from what we have come to call austerity. Flags and streamers flowered from every hand and countless periscopes — most of them little mirrors fixed on pieces of stick — danced like crystallised sunshine above the tightly packed heads.'* Philip, whom the King had created HRH The Duke of Edinburgh, Earl of Merioneth and Baron Greenwich of Greenwich a few days before, was waiting at the altar, tall and handsome in his naval uniform. Although his mother, the widowed Princess Alice was present at the wedding, Philip's sisters had not been invited. All three were married to Germans and with the war still fresh in people's memories, it was thought best that they did not attend. The ceremony was broadcast on the radio by the BBC to millions of listeners worldwide, recorded by newsreel cameras, and the 2,500 guests included six kings and seven queens. Once

Left:
14th November 1947: Mr Schur, chief confectioner at McVitie and Price, putting the final touches to the wedding cake of Princess Elizabeth and The Prince Philip, Duke of Edinburgh. The cake has four tiers and is nine feet high

Right:
Princess Elizabeth walks down the aisle of Westminster Abbey with her new husband the Duke of Edinburgh, Prince Philip

Elizabeth & Philip

Above:

The trumpeteers of the Royal Military School of Music rehearse for a fanfare to be played at Princess Elizabeth's wedding at Westminster Abbey. The fanfare has been specially composed by Sir Arnold Bax, Master of the King's Music

Left:

Princess Elizabeth in the Irish State Coach accompanied by her father HM, King George VI passes huge crowds at Trafalgar Square, on her way to marry the Duke of Edinburgh at Westminster Abbey

married, the bride having promised to obey her husband, the newly-weds left the abbey to the strains of Mendlessohn's wedding march, as the bride's parents had done 24 years earlier. The day after the wedding the bouquet was sent back to Westminster Abbey, where it was laid on the Tomb of the Unknown Warrior — the Royal Wedding tradition, started by the Princess Elizabeth's mother, Queen Elizabeth.

Back at the Palace, society photographer Barron took the official wedding portraits before 150 guests sat down to the wedding breakfast which included such dishes as *'Filets de Sole Mountbatten'* and *'Bombe Glace Princesse Elizabeth'*. Unrationed pheasant also featured on the menu. The wedding favours were individual posies of myrtle and white Balmoral heather. The string band of the Grenadier Guards played music during the breakfast and although the Royal couple received eleven wedding cakes, there was one official one which was baked by McVititie and Price, the same company who made the bride's parents' confection. Lilibet and Philip's four-tiered, nine-feet high cake used ingredients from all around the world, including sugar from the Girl Guides in Australia, which gave the cake the name *'The 10,000 Mile Cake'*. However, the meal was interrupted by the sound of 150,000 people who had broken through police barriers and were rushing towards the Palace. *'We want the bride, we want the bride!'* they were heard to chant until Lilibet and Philip went out on the balcony and greeted their ecstatic public. Two hours later, after non-stop chanting from the crowds throughout the afternoon, they repeated their balcony appearance, smiling broadly. The great British public had taken this young, clearly-in-love couple to their hearts, and playwright and actor Noel Coward wrote in his diary *'The wedding was moving and beautifully done. English tradition at its best.'*

Right:
Princess Elizabeth and the Duke of Edinburgh on honeymoon at Broadlands in Hampshire

Norman Hartnell had also created Lilibet's going away outfit. She was a vision in blue velvet as she and her husband stepped into the open Landau coach which would take them to Waterloo station, en route to the first stop of their honeymoon — Broadlands in Hampshire, the country home of Philip's uncle, Lord Louis Mountbatten. As a precaution against the chilly November evening, several hot water bottles had been tucked under the rugs covering the couple's knees while Lilibet's favourite corgi, Susan, sat at her feet. Hand-in-hand, the King and Queen came down to wave the newly-weds off while Princess Alice, Philip's mother, could be seen waving from a window. For the King, in particular, parting was such sweet sorrow. He wrote to his daughter later that evening, *'I was so proud of you and thrilled at having you so close to me on our long walk at Westminster Abbey, but when I handed your hand to the Archbishop I felt that I had lost something very precious. You were so calm and composed during the service, and said your words with such conviction, that I knew it was all right.. . . I am so glad you wrote and told mummy that you think the long wait before your engagement and the long time before the wedding was for the best. . . I can see you are sublimely happy with Philip which is right but "don't forget us" is the wish of Your ever loving and devoted Papa'*. Sublimely happy was just about right. Lilibet wrote to her mother on the day after the wedding that Philip was *'an angel'*.

When they married, both Lilibet and Philip expected to enjoy many years of happy married life before they were called upon to serve the country as Queen and Consort. Sadly, this was not to be. Just five years after their wedding day, Elizabeth, now mother to three-year-old son Charles and 18-month-old daughter Anne, became Queen at the tender age of 25, her father George VI having passed away from lung cancer at just 56. This undoubtedly put strains on the marriage but, despite their ups and downs and numerous family problems, the Queen and Prince Philip celebrated 70 years of marriage in November 2017. As she had said of her hubby in a speech 20 years before at their Golden anniversary celebration,

'He has, quite simply, been my strength and stay all these years.'

Elizabeth & Philip

'We are so happy it's unbelievable'

Margaret & Antony

MAY 6 1960

There is a pivotal scene in the second season of the Netflix award winning drama *'The Crown'* in which the newly engaged Princess Margaret discusses wedding plans with her fiancé, Antony Armstrong Jones. *'Let's do the Abbey,'* she urges. *'Let's do it bigger than my sister's. Let's eclipse her. . .'* While this is clearly a fictional account, it is without doubt a fact that Margaret's wedding did indeed outshine her sister, the Queen's. It was May 1960, rationing was long over and the war but a memory. The swinging '60s were on the horizon and according to British Prime Minister, Harold Macmillan, the country had, *'Never Had it so good.'* Certainly, a Royal Wedding had never been so lavish nor so spectacular. Margaret and Tony, as he was known, were the most attractive and glamorous royal couple in a generation, perhaps ever. They had star quality with a capital *'S'*.

There was great public enthusiasm for the match, the consensus being that Margaret deserved some happiness. Since sacrificing her former love, divorcee Group Captain Peter Townsend, for the sake of Royal duty in 1955, Margaret had seemed a little lost. In Tony, she felt she'd found herself again — or at least she seemed to have — but he was an unorthodox choice. Kings' daughters had always married princes — or dukes or earls at the very least. While Antony Armstrong Jones was undeniably upper class he was also bohemian and unconventional — a creative who took photographs for a living. For Margaret, though, that was part of the appeal.

They met in February 1958 at a small dinner party thrown by her lady-in-waiting, Lady Elizabeth Cavendish. They monopolised each other for much of the evening but it didn't occur to Margaret that Tony might be attracted to her. *'I enjoyed his company very much, but I didn't take a lot of notice of him because I thought he was queer,'* she was later to say. Margaret, like many people, assumed he was gay. But, although possibly bi-sexual, Mr Armstrong Jones was actually very much a ladies' man. They started seeing each other in secret and Margaret found herself swept up in a relationship, the like of which she'd never experienced before. Roaring around London incognito on the back of Tony's motorcycle, clandestine visits to his studio in Pimlico and to the small room he let in Bermondsey on the banks of River Thames where he would cook her supper. *'It had the most marvellous view,'* she was later to recall. *'One walked into the room and there was the river straight in front. At high tide swans looked in.'*

By and large, the couple managed to keep their relationship secret but by the summer of 1959 both the Queen and the Queen Mother were aware that Margaret was becoming more and more involved with *'the photographer'*. The Queen sensed it was serious and invited Tony up to Balmoral in early autumn. It was while he and Margaret were there together that she received a letter from Peter Townsend, informing her that he was getting engaged — to a 19-year-old Belgian girl. Although the Princess always denied that this was the spur which led her to accept Tony's proposal of marriage, it must have had some effect. However, by this stage, there is no doubt she and Tony had fallen deeply and very

passionately in love. They became privately engaged in December 1959 — the ring was a ruby surrounded by a petal-like design of diamonds. The couple were keen to make their news public but could not until the Queen had given birth to her third child, Prince Andrew, born on February 19 1960. The engagement was announced a week later on February 26 and stated, *'It is with the greatest pleasure that Queen Elizabeth the Queen Mother announces the betrothal of her beloved daughter the Princess Margaret to Mr Antony Charles Robert Armstrong-Jones. . .to which union the Queen has gladly given her consent.'* Privately, however, the Queen is thought to have had misgivings about the match. While she undoubtedly liked Tony, the upbringing and respective lifestyles of the bride and groom-to-be could not have been more different. Tony's parents had divorced when he was a child with his mother remarrying an Irish Earl while his barrister father was about to embark on his third marriage — to an air stewardess! Tony had been left to his own devices to carve the out the kind of life he wanted whereas Margaret's life had, from birth, been ruled by stiff Royal protocol and tradition. Perhaps the Queen had also heard rumours of Tony's colourful private life — on-going affairs with a dancer, an actress and possibly others. Some of Tony's own friends and family were openly against the marriage. *'Boy, you would be mad to marry Princess Margaret'* wrote his father. While his friend newspaper magnate, Jocelyn Stevens, commented that, *'Never has there been a more ill- fated assignment'*.

However, bride and groom were determined to proceed.

Immediately following the engagement announcement, made from the Royal Lodge, the Queen Mother's Windsor home, the prospective bride and groom were officially filmed and photographed together in the grounds. As soon as the last photo had been snapped, Tony was moved into Buckingham Palace. The wedding date was set for May 6 but the planning wasn't to be without problems. Tony had chosen as his best

Left & Right:
Princess Margaret and Antony Armstrong-Jones stroll the grounds of Royal Lodge in Windsor Great Park following the announcement of their engagement

man his good friend Jeremy Fry, a member of the wealthy chocolate manufacturing family. But once this was announced, it came to light that eight years earlier Fry had been convicted for a minor homosexual offence — an illegality until 1967. Given the moral climate of the time, Fry had no choice but to withdraw, citing an attack of jaundice. It was then mooted that another of Tony's friends, future leader of the Liberal Party, Jeremy Thorpe, would step into the breach. However discreet enquires into this second Jeremy's private life discovered that he, too, had homosexual leanings. Eventually Dr Roger Gilliatt, not a particularly close friend of Tony's, was selected — he was however heterosexual with no skeletons in his closet. There was further cause for concern when all but one of European royalty invited — Margaret's godmother Queen Ingrid of Denmark - declined to attend. This was surely a snub. It wasn't considered *'done'* at the time for a Royal Princess to marry a *'common'* photographer, especially one with a complicated past.

The bride put these troubles behind her and concentrated on her wedding gown. Like her elder sister, Margaret chose Norman Hartnell, saying he was *'always so good at getting the balance right'*. But she wanted something dramatically different from the heavily embroidered wedding dresses usually worn by Royal ladies. Margaret, at the suggestion of her artistic and creative husband-to-be, insisted that embellishment be kept to the absolute minimum. The finished article was stunning in its simplicity. Made from pure white silk organza, the dress featured a high collar, *'V'* neck, and fitted bodice with long sleeves made from 30 yards of sheer silk. This slim-fitting top, ballooned into a full skirt made from another 40 yards of fabric plus an eight-layer stiff tulle petticoat underneath to create the shape. It extended into a train behind. The satin bound silk tulle, cathedral length veil was made by St Cyr of Paris and the only sparkle came from the diamond necklace that had once belonged to her grandmother Queen Mary, and her tiara, the magnificent Poltimore diadem, which had been acquired for the Princess at auction for £5000 (worth over £100,000 today) and which her inner circle had christened, *'me second-best tarara'*. The Times newspaper was moved to write, *'It seems as if she moved in a soft white cloud'* while Vogue magazine commented that the gown was *'stunningly tailored'*. Margaret's wedding shoes, in a court style with a medium heel, were of white crepe and satin, and her orchid and lily-of-the-valley

May 6 dawned bright and clear. It was the perfect Spring day. Many had camped out overnight in order to secure places along the route and by the time Princess Margaret and her brother in law, The Duke of Edinburgh, who was giving her away, left Clarence House in the Glass Coach, the crowds were thought to number over 250,000. From the flagpoles along the Mall hung white silk banners with the initials 'A' and 'M' entwined on red Tudor roses, and a 60-foot floral arch of pink and red roses had been erected in front of Clarence House. So many blooms had the arch required that the city's stock of roses was completely wiped out, causing Covent Garden traders to complain that all were left were tulips. These decorations alone cost more than £20,000, the equivalent of almost half a million pounds today. There were grumblings in parliament about the cost and the Queen Mother announced that, if necessary, she would pay but in the event Prime Minister Macmillan decided that it was worth the money for the feel-good factor it had produced amongst the public.

This was to be the first televised wedding — paving the way for Royal Weddings to come. Westminster Abbey was filled with 36 cameras and three miles of electric cable to film the occasion — with emergency back-up microphones even hidden in the altar candlesticks.

The ceremony would be broadcast around the world to an estimated audience of 300 million. Meanwhile an eclectic mix of 2000 invited guests were in the Abbey - Tony's charwoman and the postman from his father's village in Wales rubbing shoulders with Prime Ministers, actresses Margaret Leighton and Joyce Grenfell and writers Jean Cocteau and John Betjeman. At 11.30 am, to the strains of hymn 'Christ is Made the Sure Foundation', the bridal procession started to make its way up the aisle and causing BBC commenter Richard Dimbleby

bouquet included the traditional sprig of myrtle. She was attended by eight young bridesmaids, including her nine-year-old niece, Princess Anne. Hartnell, at the bride's request, modelled their dresses on an early ball gown of hers of which her late father had been particularly fond. The groom was in morning dress made by tailors Denman & Goddard of Sackville Street who had fashioned his frock coats when he was an Eton schoolboy. The cherry on this particular confectionary of wedding fashion was that the principal ladies of both families wore floor-length court dress. The Queen hit the right note in a Hartnell design of turquoise blue silk taffeta and tulle.

Above Left:
Women sleeping on the Mall on the day of Princess Margaret's wedding, May 6 1960

Right:
The wedding of Princess Margaret and Lord Snowdon, Cameramen are pictured massed on Queen Victoria's statue, May 6 1960

Margaret & Antony

Abov

View of members of the British Royal family standing on the balcony at Buckingham Palace after the wedding of Princess Margaret to Antony Armstrong-Jones

Left:

Crowds line The Mall on the day of Princess Margaret's wedding to Antony Armstrong Jones

Princess Margaret and her new husband, Antony Armstrong-Jones arrive at Buckingham Palace for the wedding breakfast after their marriage at Westminster Abbey

Left:
Princess Margaret travelling to her wedding in the Glass Coach

to wax lyrically, *'For one moment we see the bride now as she looks about her in the Abbey in this lovely gown of white silk organza, with the glittering diadem on her head, the orchids in her hand, and the comforting, tall, friendly, alert figure of the Duke of Edinburgh on whose arm she can rely.'* Princess Margaret sounded calm and self-assured as she made her wedding vows, promising, as most brides did then, *'to obey'*. She made only one mistake. During the vows, she forgot to repeat the *'to have and to hold'* promise evoked by Geoffrey Fisher, the Archbishop of Canterbury, saying instead the next vow, *'For better, for worse'*. Margaret's wedding ring came from the same nugget of Welsh gold as her mother and sister's had done.

The ceremony over, the register signed and the Queen curtsied to, the new Mr and Mrs Armstrong Jones made their back way down the aisle, the cheering of the crowds growing ever louder as they emerged from the West Door. They travelled back to Buckingham Palace in the Glass Coach, the cameras following them into the palace as they arrived. The official wedding portraits were taken by Snowden's rival, Cecil Beaton, then shortly after 1pm, Tony led Margaret onto the Buckingham Palace balcony and they waved to crowds below, the cheering rising to a crescendo. At the wedding breakfast for 120 guests, the party sat down to a lunch of fillet of beef, green beans and *'soufflé surprise Montgomery'*. With the band of the Grenadier Guards outside playing Princess Margaret's favourite tunes from the musical

Right:

Princess Margaret, Countess of Snowdon, & her children, David Armstrong-Jones, Viscount Linley, and Lady Sarah Armstrong-Jones during filming of the 1969 television documentary 'Royal Family'

'Oklahoma!', Prince Philip made a short speech welcoming Tony into the family, Tony followed suite and then he and the Princess cut the six-foot wedding cake. A short while later, Margaret emerged looking stunning in a yellow silk going-away outfit and she and Tony departed the Palace in an open top Rolls Royce, having been showered with rose petals by the guests.

While the bride's mother and sister had honeymooned at stately homes in the UK, Margaret's post wedding trip was yet another break with tradition. At Tower Bridge, Tony and she were to board the Royal Yacht Britannia which would take them on a six-week Caribbean honeymoon. Such were the crowds along the way it was thought they may miss the tide. As the Princess stepped on board, her personal standard was flown, and five minutes later Britannia set off downstream. Noel Coward watching the departure on TV commented that *'it was moving and romantic and the weather still held and when Tower Bridge opened and the yacht passed through with those two tiny figures waving from just below the bridge, I discovered unashamedly and without surprise that my eyes were full of tears.'*

It was undoubtedly a magical wedding filled with joy and happiness but sadly, after the first few years, the same could not be said for the marriage. Despite the births of two children — David in 1961 and Sarah in 1964 — the hair line fissures which had always been present in the relationship, especially once the initial passion had worn off, became wide chasms. There were arguments, jealousies and infidelities on both sides and 10 years after that never-to-be forgotten wedding, Margaret and Tony, who had been created Lord Snowdon shortly before David's birth, were leading virtually separate lives. In 1976, they formally separated and two years later, divorced —

the first divorce in the British Royal family for over 400 years.

'I'm promising to "Obey" – it's traditional and I'm an old-fashioned girl'

Anne & Mark

NOVEMBER 14 1973

During the 1960s, Princess Anne, only daughter of the Queen and the Duke of Edinburgh, was a bridesmaid no fewer than four times. In January 1960, she was one of six at the wedding of her father's cousin, Lady Pamela Mountbatten. Five months later she was promoted to chief bridesmaid, overseeing seven others, on the day her Aunt Margaret wed Tony Armstrong Jones. In June 1961, as one of eight bridesmaids, she acted as chief attendant again as Miss Katherine Worsley married the Duke of Kent. And two years later, when her mother's cousin Princess Alexandra married the Honourable Angus Ogilvy, Anne was, for third time, bridesmaid-in-chief, in charge of four other attendants and two page boys. However, her maid-of-the-bride memories can't have been particularly happy ones as when she married Captain Mark Phillips at Westminster Abbey in November 1973, she refused to tolerate her own troupe of tulle-clad attendants following in her wedding day wake. She did not wish for *'yards of uncontrollable children'* as she put it, preferring, instead, just the company of her nine-year-old brother, Prince Edward, and her cousin Lady Sarah Armstrong Jones, also nine.

Anne and Mark had been secretly engaged for six weeks when the official announcement was made on May 29 1973 from Buckingham Palace. *'It is with the greatest pleasure that the Queen and Duke of Edinburgh announce the betrothal of their beloved daughter the Princess Anne to Lieutenant Mark Phillips, of the Queen's Dragoon Guards, son of Mr. and Mrs. Peter Phillips.'* The couple had become engaged at the Badminton Horse Trials, the major equestrian event in the United Kingdom, at which both Anne and Mark competed. It was their mutual love of horses that brought them together and they'd first met at the equestrian events during the 1968 Summer Olympics in Mexico City where Mark was a reserve member of the British equestrian team. Prior to their engagement, Anne and Mark competed together at both national and international events. Anne had won the individual title at the European Eventing Championship and was voted the BBC Sports Personality of the Year in 1971 when she was 21. Mark was also at the top of his game, winning the gold medal at the 1972 Munich Olympic Games as a member of the British three-day eventing team.

Despite the bride and groom's shared passion for horses — and hopefully each other, it was said that both the Queen and the Duke of Edinburgh were surprised at their daughter's choice of husband. Mark was diffident, reticent and shy while quick-witted, confident Anne always spoke her mind. Previously she'd dated more flamboyant men such as Gerald Ward, an Eton-educated ex-cavalry officer, showjumper Richard Meade and Andrew Parker-Bowles (who went on to become the first husband of Anne's future sister-in-law, the Duchess of Cornwall). It was, however, Mark's proposal she accepted. The British media searched his family tree in vain, hoping to discover some blue-blooded connection to the Princess — however remote. The best they could come up with was an ancestor, Sir John Harington, who had been Queen Elizabeth I's godson and who happened to have invented the *'water closet'*, the fore-runner of the toilet!

An official portrait of Britain's Princess Anne and Captain Mark Phillips taken 03 November 1973, one week before their wedding

Dressed in a peach-coloured silk suit complete with contrasting neckscarf and showing off her engagement ring — a large sapphire with a diamond either side made by Garrard, the Princess and her fiancé strolled around Buckingham Palace gardens on the afternoon the engagement was officially announced. While cameras had also followed Anne's parents and her Aunt Margaret and Uncle Tony around on their *'engagement days'*, this was the first time a betrothed Royal couple were seen touching — and speaking to camera. Not that they gave too much away. . . *'We're thinking mid-November for the wedding,'* said Princess Anne, *'but there are many things to be decided. There's no great rush. . .Yes it was quite a strain keeping the engagement secret. . .It's much too early to be thinking about starting a family.'* While Mark, looking decidedly nervous, revealed he'd been petrified before asking the Duke of Edinburgh for Anne's hand. *'He was very kind to me,'* the son-in-law to-be added. Both sets of parents then joined the couple on the lawn, another first for the cameras.

A few weeks later, details of the wedding were announced. It was to be on November 14, which also happened to be Prince Charles' 25th birthday, and would take place at Westminster Abbey. Meanwhile formal engagement photographs of the couple were taken at Windsor Castle

by society snapper, Norman Parkinson, and the results, it's true to say, took the nation's breath away. Parkinson had transformed the tomboy Princess into real life fairy tale one. Anne looked stunning, a vision in ultra-feminine, floor-length white lace, as she held hands with her red-jacketed handsome soldier. Her dress was by Zandra Rhodes and there were rumours that the flamboyant, pink-haired designer would also be fashioning the wedding dress. But Anne remained faithful to her favourite designer — Maureen Baker at the ready-to-wear fashion house, Susan Small.

"You will, of course, be making my wedding dress,' the Princess announced to Baker on one of her visits, shortly after the engagement had become official. The overjoyed designer drank a glass of champagne in celebration before remaining silent for months although the media offered her huge sums of money to talk about the dress. When Anne emerged on her wedding morning, it was clear that Maureen Baker had triumphed. The 23-year-old bride looked beautiful in an embroidered silk wedding dress featuring a high collar and medieval sleeves, inspired by a dress from Tudor times. Allegedly, the Princess herself came up with the idea and was keen her gown reflected court dresses from the reign of the first Queen Elizabeth. The pin-tucked bodice hugged her tiny waist while the collar and dramatic trumpet sleeves, edged in pearls and draped over chiffon cuffs, were appropriate for the required modesty of a Royal Wedding gown and also the chilly November weather. Though simple in appearance the gown, made from just one piece of silk so it was literally seamless, did have some significant ornamentation — unlike Princess Margaret's wedding dress. The neck and top featured rows of pearls, and the back and seven-foot train of the gown featured orange blossom embroidery in pearls and silver thread. In a nod to the military into which the Princess was marrying, a line of epaulettes formed from tiny pearls was just visible on each shoulder. Anne wore her hair in a slightly parted *'up-do'* which was decorated with her grandmother's famous diamond *'Sunray'* tiara — which had, of course, snapped on the bride's mother's own November wedding day 26 years before. Attached to the diadem was a long white tulle veil.

A national holiday had been declared and thousands camped out

along the route the night before the wedding despite it being bitterly cold. As with Princess Margaret's wedding, flagpoles were decorated with hangings emblazoned with the couple's entwined initials and Poet Laureate, Sir John Betjemen, penned the following verse. . .

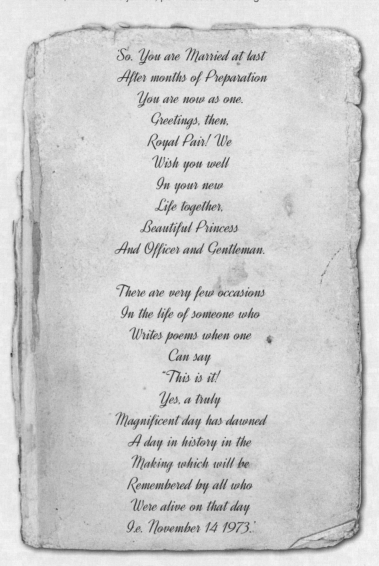

So, You are Married at last
After months of Preparation
You are now as one.
Greetings, then,
Royal Pair! We
Wish you well
In your new
Life together,
Beautiful Princess
And Officer and Gentleman.

There are very few occasions
In the life of someone who
Writes poems when one
Can say
"This is it!
Yes, a truly
Magnificent day has dawned
A day in history in the
Making which will be
Remembered by all who
Were alive on that day
I.e. November 14 1973.'

The wedding morning dawned frosty and bright. Shortly after 11 am, the Princess bride accompanied by the Duke of Edinburgh, left Buckingham Palace in the Glass Coach to deafening cheers from the crowds lining the route. Waiting for the bride and her father at the Great West Door of the Abbey were her attendants Prince Edward, dressed in Stuart tartan kilt, while Lady Sarah Armstrong Jones continued the

Right:

Princess Anne and Mark Phillips walk down the aisle together after being
married at Westminster Abbey.

Above:

Wedding Of Princess Anne To Captain Mark Phillips In Westminster Abbey

Anne & Mark

Elizabethan theme by wearing a white apron-style dress over a lattice-pattern gown, complete with Juliet cap. As the bridal party entered, a fanfare especially written for the wedding was played by trumpeters from the groom's regiment, the Queen's Dragoon Guards. The Duke of Edinburgh escorted his daughter down the aisle to the hymn *'Glorious Things of Thee Are Spoken'*. Lieutenant Phillips, wearing the full scarlet and blue uniform of his regiment and accompanied by his best man, Captain Eric Grounds, waited before the altar for his bride to arrive.

The couple were married by Michael Ramsey, Archbishop of Canterbury, watched by the 2000 guests in the Abbey and 500 million TV viewers worldwide. It was a simple ceremony from the 1662 Anglican Book of Common Prayer in which the bride promises to obey. The usual family traditions were observed. Princess Anne's ring was made from the same nugget of Welsh gold that the rings of her grandmother, her mother, and her aunt had been hewn. In her bouquet of white roses and lily-of-the-valley was the traditional sprig of myrtle.

After the ceremony, the newlyweds moved to the Edward the Confessor Chapel where the wedding register was signed. Princess Anne then made a deep curtsey to her mother while Mark respectfully bowed and the couple made their way down the aisle followed by their families as Charles-Marie Widor's *'Toccata in F Major'*, Johann Strauss' *'"Radetzky" March'* and the finale from Louis Vierne's *'Organ Symphony No.1'* were played.

On leaving the Abbey to tumultuous cheers, husband and wife travelled back to Buckingham Palace in a horse-drawn carriage, waving to the crowds as they passed. In keeping with tradition, they later appeared on the balcony of the royal residence to greet to the crowds gathered below. In addition to cheering the newly-weds, the public treated Prince Charles to several rousing renditions of *'Happy Birthday'*. At his sister's prompting, the birthday boy finally took a bow. One hundred and twenty guests sat down to a wedding breakfast or rather luncheon of lobster, partridge, followed by peppermint ice-cream. Then the bride and groom

Right:
The Wedding Of Princess Anne To Captain Mark Phillips at Westminster Abbey

cut the cake with the groom's sword — and what a cake it was. Supplied by the Royal Army Catering Corp, it measured five feet six inches — the same height as the bride, weighed 145 pounds and among its ingredients were 10 pounds each of butter and sugar, 84 eggs, 12½ pounds of flour, 70 pounds of fruit, peel, and nuts, and two bottles of brandy. The top layer featured a silver vase of flowers, the coat of arms of Princess Anne, and the regimental crest of Mark Phillips. In the background, the band of the Grenadier Guards band played *'A Bunch of Roses' and 'Bless the Bride'*. The Duke of Edinburgh, as the bride's father, toasted the health of the bride and groom with the groom's father Major Peter Phillips making the reply. In keeping with royal tradition, the Queen is said to have offered Mark an earldom on the wedding day, but he declined, making the couple's children, Peter and Zara, the first grandchildren of the sovereign to have no title.

After the wedding breakfast, Princess Anne changed into a sapphire blue velvet dress and a short-cropped jacket with mink collar and cuffs. Guests showered the couple with flower petals as they left the palace. They spent the night at White Lodge in Richmond Park and the next day flew to Barbados where they boarded the Royal Yacht Britannia. Their cruise around the Islands of the Caribbean was disrupted due to storms and high waves and for most of the first week, the couple suffered from seasickness. Eventually, the storms subsided and the newlyweds could enjoy their trip. The couple ended their honeymoon in the Galapagos Islands in the Pacific Ocean.

Anne and Mark remained happily married for several years. Peter, was born in November 1978, followed by Zara in May 1981. However, before the '80s were out, Anne and Mark had formally separated, with rumours of affairs on both sides.

The Princess' second marriage in 1992 couldn't have been more different from her first.

Anne & Mark

Above:

Princess Anne on her wedding day with her husband Mark Phillips, her younger brother Prince Edward, and cousin Lady Sarah Armstrong-Jones

Right & Next page:

Princess Anne and Mark Phillips on the balcony of Buckingham Palace following their wedding with other members of the Royal family

Anne & Mark

Anne and Timothy

Anne, made Princess Royal by her mother in 1987, met Royal Navy Commander Timothy Laurence when he was Equerry to the Queen over a three-year period. During this time, he learned the ways of the Royal Family — often eating with them, accompanying them on outings and making formal introductions when important guests came to visit. Anne's marriage to Mark Phillips was in trouble and Timothy caught her eye. However, it was not until 1989, when four of Timothy's love letters were stolen from Anne's briefcase at Buckingham Palace, that the romance came to light. In the same year, Anne separated from her first husband, but the courtship with Timothy remained discreet. The couple was seldom seen together until Anne's divorce became final in April 1992.

The couple's intention to marry was announced by Buckingham Palace on December 5 1992, just a week before the wedding. A Palace spokesperson said, *'Due to the level of speculation about the matter, we decided to confirm that The Princess Royal and Commander Laurence are planning to marry, but I cannot say where and when.'* Anne's second engagement ring was another sapphire — this time a round-cut or cabochon stone surrounded by three small diamonds on either side.

The small, private wedding was held on December 12 1992, at the tiny church in Crathie, Scotland, close to the Balmoral Estate. The couple chose to marry in Scotland as the Church of England did not at that time allow divorced persons whose former spouses were still living to remarry in its churches. Princess Anne arrived at Crathie Church accompanied by her father Prince Philip and her 11-year-old daughter Zara who acted as her bridesmaid. Anne was dressed in a simple white suit with white blossoms in her hair and Timothy was wearing his Royal Navy uniform. Before about 30 guests, the bride and groom exchanged vows to stay together *'until God shall separate us by death'.* After the ceremony, the newlyweds emerged from the church to the accompaniment of pipers and the cheers of approximately 500 well-wishers. Press and photographers were barred from the church but they lined the road from Balmoral Castle to Crathie Church. After the wedding, the newlyweds and their guests had a short champagne celebration at Craigowan Lodge on the Balmoral Estate. A two-day honeymoon at the castle followed.

In December 2017, Princess Anne and Sir Timothy (he was knighted by his mother-in-law in 2011) celebrated 25 years of marriage.

'Here is the stuff of which fairy tales are made'

Charles & Diana

JULY 29 1981

Two million spectators lining the route, 750 million more worldwide watching on TV, 4000 police and 2200 military officers managing the crowds. . . Three-and-half thousand invited guests (including most of the crowned heads of Europe, leading world figures and dignitaries), 12 trumpeters, four choirs, six officiating clergy, one world-class soprano, and three orchestras. . . all decanted into the baroque splendour of Christopher Wren's iconic St Paul's Cathedral. There has never been a Royal Wedding so filled with pomp and ceremony, grandeur and magnificence, and pure unadulterated majesty as the nuptials between HRH Prince Charles and the Lady Diana Spencer. It is extremely unlikely there will ever be again. Dubbed the *'Wedding of the Century'*, it would, perhaps, be more apt to call it the *'Wedding of the Millennium'.*

The wedding of the heir to the throne was always going to be a lavish affair — the country had been chomping at the bridal bit since Charles had announced, a few years earlier, that 30 would be a good age to settle down. He turned 30 in November 1978. The problem was finding a suitable mate. The love of his life, Camilla Shand, had married Andrew Parker Bowles in 1973 when Charles dithered about making a commitment — not that Camilla had been deemed *'suitable'*. She had too much of a past. The requirements were as follows — a girl from an aristocratic family who had no salacious skeletons in the closet. In other words, a virgin with no sexual past. The pressure was on so when, in the summer of 1980, the young Lady Diana Spencer, daughter

of the eighth Earl Spencer, caught Charles' eye aged just 19, it looked very promising indeed. Diana ticked every box. Charles had known her for several years and had once dated her elder sister, Lady Sarah. He first took a serious interest in Diana as a potential bride when they were guests at a barbeque in the country. He then invited her for a sailing weekend to Cowes aboard the royal yacht Britannia. This was followed by an invitation to Balmoral where Diana was well received by the family. The couple then had several dates in London. Diana and Charles had been seeing each other for about six months — but had only been on about 12 or 13 dates in all — when he proposed on February 3 1981 in the nursery at Windsor Castle. Diana burst into giggles but promptly accepted. In true Royal tradition, the engagement was kept secret for the next few weeks.

This official engagement announcement, issued by Buckingham Palace at 11 am on February 24 1981, ended years of speculation over who the world's most eligible bachelor would marry. *'It is with the greatest pleasure that The Queen and The Duke of Edinburgh announce the betrothal of their beloved son, The Prince of Wales, to the Lady Diana Spencer, daughter of the Earl Spencer and the Honourable Mrs. Shand Kydd.'* Diana selected an elegant, £30,000 engagement ring — the most expensive in the Garrard catalogue, consisting of 14 solitaire diamonds, surrounding a 12-carat oval blue Ceylon sapphire set in 18-carat white gold. Following tradition, the couple posed for their first official appearance on the terrace at the rear of Buckingham Palace with Diana wearing a sapphire blue suit and white silk blouse with a blue swallow motif, hastily

with diamonds winking away at her ears and throat. It was Snowdon who also snapped a more informal image of the couple — the most informal royal engagement photo taken up till then — of Diana standing behind Charles with her arms possessively wrapped around him while he leaned against her, smiling proudly.

Wednesday July 29 was chosen as the day for the Royal Wedding-to-end-all-Royal Weddings. As the date, which had been proclaimed a national holiday, approached excitement reached fever pitch. Tens of thousands of street parties were organised up and down and across the country with Brits turning their roads, streets, avenues and cul-de-sacs into bunting-festooned party zones. The wedding was to take place at St Paul's rather than the more traditional Westminster Abbey as the famous domed cathedral could accommodate 1500 more guests in addition to being the perfect venue for the joyous musical extravaganza Prince Charles so desired. Historically, too, it was a fitting choice — the only other Royal Wedding to ever have taken place at St Paul's was that between Arthur, Prince of Wales, eldest son of Henry VII, and Catherine of Aragon, in 1501.

It wouldn't come out till many years later but secretly both bride and groom were having second thoughts about the marriage. Diana was finding it difficult adjusting to the confines of Royal Life but she also had deep concerns about Charles' involvement with Camilla Parker Bowles. She seriously considered calling the wedding off. *'Bad luck, Duch,'* said her sisters, Jane and Sarah, calling her by her family nickname. *'Your face is on the tea-towels so you're too late to chicken out.'* Charles, meanwhile, was reportedly in tears the night before the wedding, wondering if he was doing the right thing. *'It would,'* quoted one source, *'have taken a very, very brave man to call it off at that late stage.'*

purchased from Harrods. The nation promptly fell in love with this young English rose who smiled shyly and coyly tilted her head to one side while casting her big blue eyes endearingly downwards. Not yet 20 while her husband-to-be was 12 years older, there were already signs, however, that perhaps this wasn't a match made in heaven. *'You're very much in love?'* questioned the TV interviewer. *'Of course,'* Diana replied without hesitation. *'Whatever in love means. . .'* added Charles.

Diana was promptly moved out of the flat she shared with three friends and into Clarence House, the Queen Mother's London residence. It was here, it was supposed, she would learn the regal ropes. In one official engagement photograph by one-time Royal consort, Lord Snowden, she looked the part already — majestic in moss green taffeta

Above Left:
Lady Diana Spencer reveals her sapphire and diamond engagement ring while she and Prince Charles pose for photographs in the grounds of Buckingham Palace following the announcement of their engagement

Above Right:
Chief Petty Officer cook David Avery with the Royal wedding cake made for Prince Charles and Princess Diana's wedding, 29th July 1981

No one who witnessed that late July day in 1981 will ever forget it. As dawn broke, vast crowds already lined the patriotically-decorated streets of London. Guests started arriving at St. Paul's Cathedral as soon as the doors opened at 9am and were greeted with cheers from well-wishers. Meanwhile at Clarence House, Diana was preparing for the biggest day of her life. Her dress was the creation of a husband and wife team of designers, David and Elizabeth Emmanuel, who specialised in deeply romantic styles and were influenced by the likes of actress Vivien Leigh as Scarlett O'Hara in *'Gone with The Wind'*. Diana's wedding gown was the ultimate 1980s *'meringue'*. Made of ivory pure silk taffeta with embroidered lace panels at the front and back of the bodice, it had puffy lace-flounced sleeves and a neckline decorated with taffeta bows. The train was twenty-five feet long — the longest Royal bridal train in history — and was made of silk taffeta trimmed with sparkling old lace. Both the dress and the ivory silk tulle veil were hand-embroidered with thousands of mother-of-pearl sequins and pearls, as were the matching silk slippers. A little blue bow and a tiny gold horseshoe were sewn into the waist of the dress for good luck. Diana's *'borrowed'* and *'old'* items were the Spencer family tiara which secured the veil and her mother's diamond earrings, respectively. Her bouquet was a trailing arrangement of orchids, stephanotis, gardenias, lilies of the valley, freesias, gold Mountbatten roses and, naturally, the traditional sprig of myrtle.

The 600,000 crowds thronging London's streets had already witnessed the processions of senior members of the Royal Family, including the bride groom and his two supporters — brothers Andrew and Edward — when Diana and her father, Earl Spencer, emerged from the grounds of Clarence House onto the Mall in the Glass Coach. At the first sight of their Fairy-tale Princess, a huge roar went up that continued all the way to St Paul's — almost three miles away. Diana's five bridesmaids — including Charles' cousin Lady Sarah Armstrong Jones (17), Charles' god daughter India Hicks (14), and five-year-old Clementine Hambro, the great, great grand-daughter of Sir Winston Churchill, were waiting for her on the steps of St Pauls, all dressed in flouncy Emmanuel creations of their own. As the bride emerged from the coach, her dress was so voluminous it appeared creased and required a swift straightening by her eldest bridesmaid. The two page boys, Lord Nicholas Windsor (11) and eight-year-old Edward van Cutsem, both dressed in both dressed in Royal Navy cadet summer uniforms dating from 1863 which was the

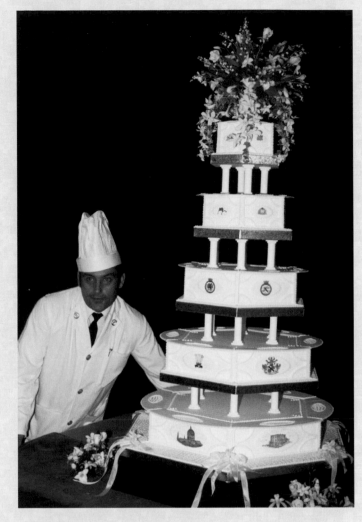

date of the last State Wedding of a Prince of Wales, joined the bridal party. They were ready to go. As Diana entered the cathedral on her father's arm, the State Trumpeters of the Household Cavalry sounded a fanfare and she made her three-and-a-half-minute walk up the aisle to the accompaniment of *'Trumpet Voluntary"* by Jeremiah Clark.

Although Diana was later to say that she was distracted looking for Camilla Parker Bowles in the congregation as she walked down the aisle, there's no doubt she was overwhelmed by the majesty of the occasion. *'There were several times when I was perilously close to crying from the sheer joy of it all. It was heaven, amazing, wonderful,'* she was later quoted as saying. Waiting for her was Charles, handsome in the Navy's No. 1 ceremonial dress uniform with a blue Garter sash. *'I remember*

Above:
Princess Diana and Prince Charles walking down the aisle of St Paul's in London on their wedding day with their bridesmaids and pageboys

Right:
Lady Diana Spencer, wearing an Emanuel wedding dress, prepares to enter St. Paul's Cathedral on the arm of her father, Earl Spencer, for her wedding to Prince Charles, Prince of Wales

Charles & Diana

being so in love with my husband that I couldn't take my eyes off him. I just absolutely thought I was the luckiest girl in the world,' she was to recall. The service began with a hymn. Charles chose *'Christ Is Made the Sure Foundation.'* Later came Diana's choice — *'I Vow to Thee My Country'* which she'd loved since schooldays. The Dean of St. Paul's introduced the service, but Robert Runcie, the Archbishop of Canterbury, performed the ceremony. In a break with tradition, Diana chose not to *'obey'* her husband. Mistakes were made during the vows. Diana vowed to take *'Philip Charles Arthur George'* as her legally married husband rather than the correct *'Charles Philip Arthur George',* and Charles vowed to share all his wife's worldly goods rather than his own. The wedding band was from the same nugget of gold that had provided the rings of the Queen Mother, the Queen, Princess Margaret, and Princess Anne. Towards the end of the 75 minute ceremony, the Archbishop of Canterbury announced to the congregation that, *'Here is the stuff of which fairy tales are made: the Prince and Princess on their wedding day. Those who are married live happily ever after the wedding day if they persevere in the real adventure which is the task of creating each other and creating a more loving world.'*

After signing the register, the couple returned to the altar as Dame Kiri Te Kanawa sang Handel's *'Let the Bright Seraphim'.* Diana gave a deep curtsey to the Queen before walking back down the aisle to the strain of *'Pomp and Circumstance March No. 4 in G'* and *'Crown Imperial.'* The bells of St. Paul's began to peal in celebration as the newly-weds arrived at the Great Door and a massive cheer went up from the waiting crowds. The couple, their faces wreathed in smiles, climbed inside the 1902 State Postillion Landau carriage and began the journey back to Buckingham Palace, taking in Ludgate Hill, Fleet Street, the Law Courts, the Strand, Trafalgar Square, and then onto The Mall.

Once inside the Palace, the official wedding portraits were taken by the Queen's cousin, society snapper Patrick Lichfield. Then came the eagerly anticipated balcony appearances. There were five in all plus, at the bidding of the crowds below, Charles finally kissed his

bride — the first kiss ever publicly shared by Royal newly-weds. The wedding breakfast followed — a banquet of brill coated in lobster sauce, *'supreme de volaille'*, and *'Princesse de Galles strawberries and cream',* served with three different wines. The five-tiered, 225-pound hexagonal wedding cake was cut by Prince Charles, using his ceremonial sword. Made by the Royal Navy Cookery School in Chatham, it had taken 11 weeks to create, including etching the couple's coats of arms, family crests, and pictures of their homes — in colour — onto the white icing. A few hours later, Charles and Diana left Buckingham Palace in an open carriage decorated with heart-shaped balloons sporting imprints of the Prince of Wales' feathers, and a *'Just Married'* sign scrawled in lipstick borrowed from a lady-in-waiting which were placed there by Prince Andrew and Prince Edward. Charles had changed into a grey suit and Diana into a peach-coloured silk suit designed by Belville Sassoon and matching hat by Knightsbridge milliner John Boyd. She was also wearing the same six-strand pearl choker that her sister Sarah had worn to the wedding. Sarah went home bare-necked while her younger sister and new brother-in-law took another carriage ride to Waterloo Station, cheered by crowds who still thronged the pavements.

In a nod to Royal Weddings of the past Charles and Diana took the Royal train to Broadlands where the Queen and Prince Philip had spent their wedding night in 1947. After three days of peace and quiet, they flew from Eastleigh Airport to Gibraltar where the couple boarded the Royal Yacht Britannia for a Mediterranean cruise. After two weeks, the couple flew to Scotland to join the rest of the Royal Family at Balmoral until the autumn. By the end of their extended honeymoon, Diana was pregnant with Prince William — and the union was, as was later revealed, already in trouble. After 11 years of largely unhappy marriage with infidelities and scandal on both sides,

the Wales' formally separated in 1992 and divorced four years later.

Charles & Diana

Above:
Spectators waiting outside Buckingham Palace for the wedding
procession

Right:
Crowds outside Buckingham Palace in London

Charles & Diana

Charles & Diana

Charles & Camilla

Diana was tragically killed in a car accident in 1997 — before she was able to achieve any kind of *'Happy Ever After'*. There was one for her ex-husband, however. He became engaged to love-of-his-life, the now divorced Camilla Parker Bowles, on February 10 2005, and presented her with a ring that had belonged to his beloved granny, the late Queen Mother, who had passed away three years earlier. In a 1920s-style platinum setting, the ring was composed of a square-cut central diamond flanked by six diamond baguettes,

In another first for Royal Weddings the marriage ceremony, on April 9, was actually a civil ceremony, taking place at Windsor register office with only the couple's closest family members in attendance. However, the Queen did not attend. The bride wore a delicate cream silk chiffon dress with a matching oyster silk basket weave coat while her groom was dressed in morning suit.

For the blessing at St George's Chapel (which the Queen did go to), Camilla adopted a more formal look — a floor length pale blue chiffon dress embroidered with gold detail, a matching coat of blue and gold damask, and stunning headdress fashioned from golden feathers.

Following the reception — a lavish traditional tea, including egg and cress sandwiches, mini Cornish pasties and boiled fruit cake — the Queen made a touching speech. She began by saying she had two important announcements to make. The first was that her horse Hedgehunter had won the race at Aintree, the second that she was delighted to be welcoming her son and his bride to the *'winners' enclosure'*. Her Majesty continued, *'They have overcome Beecher's Brook and The Chair and all kinds of other terrible obstacles. They have come through and I'm very proud and wish them well. My son is home and dry with the woman he loves.'* Camilla, now the Duchess of Cornwall, is said to have felt her mother-in-law's words were an indication that she was now fully accepted into the family fold. After the wedding, Princes William and Harry scrawled *'Prince + Duchess'* on the windscreen of their father's car. The newly-weds honeymooned in the Scottish Highlands.

Above:

Prince of Wales, Prince Charles and the Duchess of Cornwall, Camilla Parker-Bowles, inside St George's Chapel in Windsor Castle for the Service of Prayer and Dedication for their marriage blessing

'Our Wedding Was So Perfect'

Andrew and Sarah

JULY 23 1986

While the 1981 wedding between Prince Charles and Lady Diana Spencer was without doubt the grandest, most spectacular Royal Wedding of modern times, when it comes to pure feel-good factor and a sense of relaxed yet unadulterated joy, the wedding between the Sailor Prince Andrew and fun-loving, flame-haired Sarah Ferguson five years later was, as the groom himself said, *'So perfect'.*

The courtship, engagement and wedding was pretty much a whirlwind affair - all happening within a period of just 13 months. Andrew and Sarah, whose father Major Ron Ferguson was Prince Charles' polo manager, had played together as children but it was Andrew's sister-in-law, the Princess of Wales, also a friend of Sarah's, who engineered the romance. She saw to it that Sarah received an invitation to lunch at Windsor before attending Royal Ascot in June 1985. *'We were made to sit next to each other,'* Andrew was to later recall. *'Yes,'* demurred Sarah. *'He made me eat chocolate profiteroles which I didn't want to eat at all.'* A rowdy food fight ensued with these two individuals perhaps recognising a kindred spirit in the other.

At 25 years of age, both Andrew and Sarah, known as *'Fergie'*, were looking for a life partner with whom to settle down. Andrew's last serious relationship with *'unsuitable'* American actress Koo Stark had ended a few years earlier due, in large part, to pressure from the Royal Family. Sarah, until she became romantically involved with the Prince, had been dating much older motor racing entrepreneur, Paddy McNally, for several years but he had made it very clear that he wasn't interested in marriage. After

the *'Profiteroles'* incident, Andrew and Sarah went on a number of under-the-radar dates. As the romance progressed, Andrew presented Sarah with a Russian wedding ring, a pre-engagement symbol amongst young aristos to state *'one was spoken for'.* The Queen invited Sarah to stay at Sandringham that New Year where she was photographed holding hands with Her Majesty's second son but it was during a stay at Floors Castle in Scotland, the home of Andrew's good friends, the Duke and Duchess of Roxburghe, that Andrew popped the question. The date was February 19 1986 — his 26th birthday. Going down on both knees, he asked Sarah to marry him. She accepted without hesitation but gave him a *'get-out-of-jail-free'* card. *'When you wake up tomorrow morning, you can tell me it's a huge joke,'* she said. The Prince, however, was serious.

The official announcement could not be made until the Queen and the Duke of Edinburgh returned from their tour of Australasia. Once home, Her Majesty gave the match her blessing and on March 19 1986, the following statement was released from Buckingham Palace — *'It is with great pleasure that the Queen and the Duke of Edinburgh announce the betrothal of their beloved son the Prince Andrew to Miss Sarah Ferguson, daughter of Maj. Ronald Ferguson and Mrs. Hector Barrantes'.*

As both Anne and Mark, and Charles and Diana had done, the newly engaged Andrew and Sarah took a stroll in the Buckingham Palace gardens. Sarah, wearing a blue suit by designer Alistair Blair, proudly showed off her engagement ring, made by the crown jewellers, Garrard (who else?) from sketches Andrew had himself drawn. Completed in just

Above:

Proud parents Queen Elizabeth II and Prince Philip riding in an open carriage en-route to Westminster Abbey for the wedding of their son Prince Andrew to Miss Sarah Ferguson

Right:

Ceremonial Welsh Guards troops line the parade route during the Royal Wedding of Prince Andrew to Sarah Ferguson

Andrew & Sarah

under a week, it was dominated by a Burmese ruby, chosen to match the bride-to-be's Titian tresses, which was surrounded by 10 drop diamonds. *'We're good friends — a good team. We're very happy,'* the couple told the TV cameras. For the official engagement photographs, cockney boy-turned-fashion photographer Terence Donovan was chosen. Although he had never photographed Royalty before, the results were stunning. The happy couple stood side by side in one of the State Rooms at Buckingham Palace, the Prince wearing the ceremonial day dress uniform of a naval lieutenant, while his bride in an elegant three-tiered satin evening dress in white, black and royal blue, looked positively regal. But then Sarah did have Royal blood, albeit from the wrong side of the sheets. Like the Duchess of Cornwall and the late Diana, Princess of Wales, Sarah is descended from King Charles II via his illegitimate children — Charles Lennox, 1st Duke of Richmond, son of Charles II and his mistress Louise de Kérouaille, Duchess of Portsmouth; and James Scott, 1st Duke of Monmouth, son of Charles II and his mistress Lucy Walter.

The wedding date was set for July 23 1986, a Wednesday, although unlike the respective nuptials of Princess Anne and Prince Charles, it was not proclaimed a national holiday. There was, however, a real holiday atmosphere in the run up to the big day. Fergie, Princess Diana and comedienne Pamela Stephenson, all disguised as policewomen, attempted to crash Andrew's Stag or Bachelor Party, an exclusive dinner for 20 of the Prince's closest friends at a Kensington mansion. When they didn't succeed, they ended up in Annabel's nightclub and sipped cocktails — until they were rumbled. This light-hearted atmosphere continued as the wedding party went to the Abbey to rehearse the Big Day. Prince Edward, Andrew's younger brother and *'supporter'*, who had flown in from New Zealand for the ceremony, arrived with his arm in a sling as a gag, claiming to have been *'bitten by a kiwi'*. A thoroughly relaxed Fergie kicked off her shoes and slipped behind an Abbey piano for an impromptu recital. Then there was the pre-wedding party thrown by Major Ferguson at Smith's Lawn in Windsor Great Park for 700 guests, including actor Michael Caine,

ex-race car champion Jackie Stewart, and pop superstar Elton John.

Sarah spent the night before the wedding at Clarence House. Well-wishers were already camped out along the Mall. Before she went to bed, Sarah slipped out to absorb some of the atmosphere, although she beat a hasty retreat once she'd been recognised. The next morning, hair and make-up done, she was helped into her wedding gown by its designer, the little known Lindka Cierach. Of the dress, Sarah had said that *'there will never be another like it'*. She was right. Cierach created a classic, Edwardian-style dress made from heavy ivory satin which featured a deeply scooped neckline, fitted bodice which emphasised Sarah's waist, three-quarter length slightly puffed sleeves with bows at the shoulder and a full skirt. The bodice of the dress was beautifully hand embroidered with intricate beadwork while the 17-and-half foot train featured intertwined *'A'* and *'S'* initials for the bridal couple's names, ship anchors and waves to honour Prince Andrew's naval career, and bumblebees and thistles from Sarah's newly-created Ferguson family crest. Sewn into the underskirt of the gown were several blue bows containing good-luck messages from her family. Her shoes were covered in beaded duchess satin which matched her dress. She wore her red hair long and in loose curls, and her bridal veil, made of pure silk and embroidered with hearts and sequins, was attached to a coronet of flowers — lily of the valley, cream roses, gardenias and cream lily petals. She carried a lovely S-shaped bouquet made of gardenias, cream lilies, yellow roses, lilies of the valley and the traditional sprig of myrtle. Sarah's four small bridesmaids, one of whom was Andrew's five-year-old neice, Zara Phillips, wore Cierach-designed dresses of peach taffeta silk trimmed in peach cotton lace and beautiful floral headdresses. Her four pages whose number included Peter Phillips and the four-year-old Prince William wore midshipmen and sailors uniforms of the Royal Navy from 1782, complete with sailor hats.

Tens of thousands lined the mile-long route from Buckingham Palace to Westminster Abbey while 800 million more across the globe watched on TV. As Sarah and her father Major Ronald Ferguson left Clarence House in the Glass Coach, the sun started to shine. At the Abbey, a trumpet fanfare announced the arrival of the bridal party. After a quick adjustment to the train and veil, Sarah beamed, as on her father's arm, she made her way past 1800 guests, to the strains of Elgar's Imperial March. *'Come on, dads,'* she is

Andrew & Sarah

Above:
Prince Andrew together with his bride Sarah Ferguson wave from the
carriage at it departs Westminster Abbey

Right:
The Royal Wedding of Prince Andrew and Sarah, Duchess of York on July
23 1986 in London. The Royal couple returning down The Mall from St.
Pauls Cathedral in an open carriage to Buckingham Palace

Andrew & Sarah

rumoured to have said as they started off. *'Let's show 'em how it's done.'*

Her Prince, supported by younger brother Edward, and wearing the dress uniform of a Royal Navy lieutenant complete with a sword at his side, was waiting for her in the Abbey chancel, where he was seen to mouth *'You look wonderful'*. *'Thank you, darling,'* she whispered back. The only sign of nerves on Sarah's part came when she repeated 'Christian', one of

Above:
The Royal couple playfully listening to the crowd outside Buckingham Palace calling for them to kiss

Right:
The Duke and Duchess of York kissing on the Buckingham Palace balcony after their wedding

his groom's middle names. Andrew, meanwhile, seemed to have difficulty slipping the band of Welsh gold onto his bride's finger. Unlike her sister-in-law, Diana, Sarah chose to obey her new husband. She had given her reason why during a pre-wedding interview. *'Since he is going to be worshipping, I chose to obey deliberately. Someone is going to have to make the decisions. Let the man make the final decision. But I was thinking of obeying in moral terms as opposed to physically obeying. I am not the sort of woman who is going to meekly trot along behind her husband. I am not a person to obey meekly. When I want to, I will stress a point.'*

Having signed the register in the Chapel of Edward the Confessor, the newly-weds emerged. They were now the Duke and Duchess of York, the Queen having conferred the title on her second son at 10 am that morning. As be-fitted her new Royal Status, Sarah had removed the floral headdress and replaced it with a diamond tiara which her mother-in-law had purchased for her from Garrard. Having paid homage to their sovereign —

although Sarah almost forgot to curtsy — the bride and groom made their way back down the aisle. Like all Royal brides, the Duchess arranged to have her bouquet laid on the tomb of the unknown soldier. They emerged from the Abbey at just before 12.30pm and the waiting crowds went wild.

Returning to Buckingham Palace, having travelled back in a 1902 State Landau, the new Duke and Duchess were taken off for the official photographs. *'Vogue'* photographer Albert Watson had been chosen to take the images and had just 25 minutes to complete his task. He attracted the attention of various Windsor and Ferguson family members by squeezing on an old-fashioned hooter. At one point, Watson realised one of the principal people was missing. *'I looked round to see the Queen being helped up a ladder by my assistant so she could look through the camera herself,'* he was to reveal. Official photos taken, the bridal party headed onto the famous balcony. As soon as the 10,000-strong crowd saw the newly-weds, they started chanting, *'We want a kiss! We want a kiss!'* Sarah playfully pretended she couldn't hear but then, leaning towards her new husband, enthusiastically kissed him.

Running late now, 140 guests then sat down in the State Supper Room to three sumptuous courses — Eggs Drumkilbo (hard-boiled egg moulded with lobster, prawns and mayonnaise — thought to be the Queen Mother's favourite), lamb with mint sauce, and strawberries and cream in the shape of the St George's cross. The toasts were made in Bollinger champagne. Close to 4.30pm, Andrew and Sarah (now changed out of their wedding finery and into a grey lounge suit and a multi-coloured floral print dress, respectively) left the Palace in a horse-drawn carriage, decorated with a giant teddy bear and foil balloons. As the carriage drove off the Queen and other members of the Royal Family were caught on camera, laughing and trying to chase the carriage. Arriving at Royal Hospital Chelsea, the couple took a red Wessex Helicopter of the Queen's Flight to Heathrow where they boarded a jet heading for the Azores, their honeymoon destination.

Two years after they tied the knot, the couple welcomed their first child born at the Portland Hospital in London on Aug 8 1988. Then, on March

23, 1990, her younger sister Princess Eugenie Victoria Helena of York was born. But in January 1992 — six years after their lavish wedding and two years after the arrival of their youngest child — Sarah and Andrew decided to separate. Sarah has since said she believes the marriage started to break down just one week after the Westminster ceremony because of her husband's naval duties. After four years of separation, the couple made the mutual decision to divorce. Their marriage officially came to an end on May 30, 1996. Neither has remarried, they continue to share a home and there are rumours that one day they may even remarry. They are according to Sarah,

'The happiest divorced couple in the world'.

Edward & Sophie

In contrast to the nuptials of his siblings, the wedding of Prince Edward to Public Relations consultant Sophie Rees-Jones on June 19 1999 was a deliberately low-key affair. The previous 10 years had been particularly traumatic for the Royal family what with the divorces of the Queen's three elder children, countless scandals, revelations of infidelity, the fire which almost destroyed Windsor Castle and the death of the Princess of Wales. It was felt that the public had lost their appetite for spectacular Royal Weddings — especially when odds were the marriages would only end in divorce.

On January 6 1999 Prince Edward held a press conference to announce he and Sophie Rhys-Jones were engaged. Their relationship had begun six years earlier and the Prince asked Ms. Rhys-Jones to marry him over the 1998 Christmas holidays. In accepting the Prince's proposal, Sophie also accepted an exquisite engagement ring — a cluster of three diamonds set in white gold. The Prince said that while the love affair was not a sudden strike of lightning, he and Sophie were very much in love.

The wedding ceremony took place at St George's Chapel Windsor, a smaller, less showy and more private venue than St Pauls Cathedral or Westminster Abbey. Several Royal Wedding traditions were to be broken at this wedding. The service took place in the late afternoon rather than late morning and invitations stipulated that female guests wore long dresses with covered shoulders, and no hats. No carriages nor state coaches transported the principal persons to the chapel. The bride and her father, and the Queen and the Duke of Edinburgh travelled by Rolls Royce, while the groom and his supporters — brothers Charles and Andrew — walked from the Castle. All other guests arrived by minibus.

Sophie's gown was relatively simple — an ivory silk crepe corseted coat over an ivory silk organza skirt — but it sparkled with 325,000 hand sewn cut-glass and pearl beads. She wore a silk tulle veil one inch longer than her train, which was dotted with crystal beads, and supported by a diamond tiara borrowed from the Queen's private collection. Her shoes were also ivory silk crepe, and her bouquet consisted of ivory garden roses, stephanotis, lily of the valley, freesia — and the obligatory sprig of myrtle. She also wore a black and white pearl necklace and matching earrings designed by Prince Edward as a personal wedding gift. The Prince looked handsome in formal morning dress, with a yellow waistcoat, blue shirt with white collar and a patterned blue and yellow tie. He, too, wore his wedding gift from his beloved — a gold pocket watch and chain. Their four small attendants were in medieval-themed dress.

As the clock struck 5pm, the bride and her father made their way up the aisle of St George's Chapel. A forty-five-minute ceremony followed, after which the new Earl and Countess of Wessex rode in an open carriage to the reception at Windsor Castle, greeting thousands of well-wishers who had come out to celebrate their marriage.

The marriage is now in its 19th year.

'We're supposed to have just a small family affair'

William & Catherine

APRIL 29 2011

On April 29 2011 at approximately 11.35am, Prince William of Wales and second in line to the British throne, stood before the altar at Westminster Abbey, about to be married to Miss Catherine Middleton in what was the most important Royal Wedding since that of his parents, 30 years earlier. There were 1900 guests inside the ancient, awe-inspiring Abbey — the absolute antithesis of the small family affair William had joked to his bride's father about but perhaps there had been a modicum of wishful thinking in the comment. The family he was marrying into — the Berkshire-based, middle class Middletons — were almost as important to him as his own blue-hued blood relations. While he undoubtedly loved Catherine, or Kate as she is popularly known, her warm, loving, extremely close family who had welcomed him into their home, was an added bonus. For William, who famously came from a broken home (or rather homes), and who lost his mother when he was just 15, this kind of family life was something he'd yearned for.

William and Kate's courtship had been pretty standard in real life terms but maybe not so much in Royal. They met as first year students at the University of St Andrews in Scotland in September 2001 and became friends. But friendship blossomed into romance when William saw Kate modelling a see-through dress at a student fashion show in March 2002, prompting him to murmur to a friend, *'Wow, Kate's hot!'* Their relationship continued throughout university, surviving the odd rough patch as William momentarily had his head turned by a number of aristocratic

beauties during the holidays. The couple set up home together in their final year and following graduation in 2005, both left Scotland.

William had decided on a military career and so went to Sandhurst while Kate moved to London and began working as an accessories buyer for a fashion store. Their relationship continued to thrive despite the separations but then over Easter 2007, they split. There had been speculation about them marrying for months, with shop-chain Woolworths even going so far as to launch a range of *'Kate and William Royal Wedding'* souvenirs. William felt tied down and wanted to play the field before settling down. Many women in her position would have gone underground but not Kate. Determined to show William just what he was missing, she went out on the town, making sure she looked gorgeous and like she was having a ball. Her plan worked. Within a matter of months, William and Kate secretly started seeing each other again — once Kate had decided to give him a second chance, that is. By the close of 2007, Kate had moved into William's apartment in Clarence House but she needed reassurance that she was *'the one'*. William was happy to provide this, although he stressed he was not yet ready for marriage. Three years on, however, he was.

In October 2010, Kate and William were enjoying a holiday in Kenya. Unbeknown to her, he had in his rucksack the iconic sapphire and diamond engagement ring that had belonged to his mother. On the last day of their three-week trip, he got down on one knee and proposed. Kate accepted, saying later, *'It was very romantic. I didn't really expect*

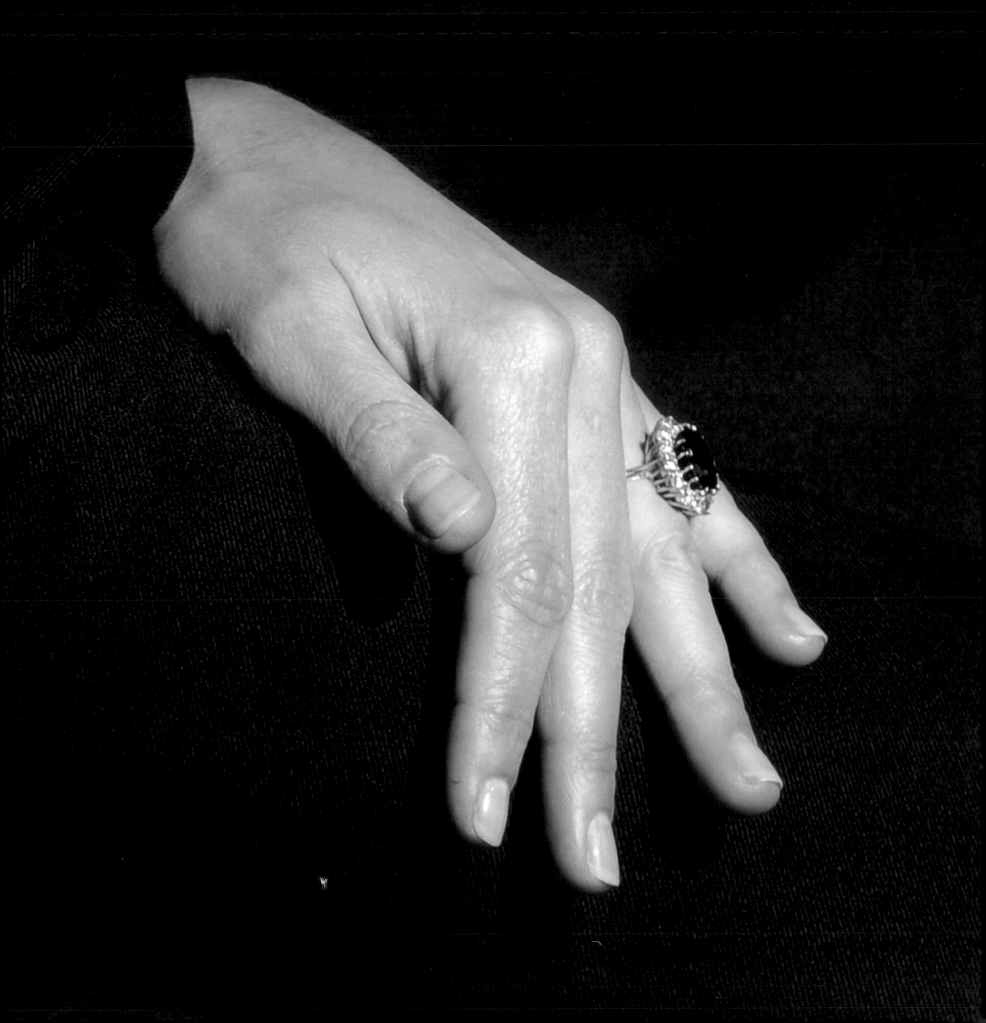

it. It was a total shock. . .and very exciting.' The engagement remained secret for almost a month but on November 16, the announcement finally came. *'His Royal Highness Prince William of Wales and Miss Catherine Middleton are engaged to be married,'* it read. *'The Prince of Wales is delighted to announce the engagement of Prince William to Miss Catherine Middleton. The wedding will take place in the spring or summer of 2011 in London.'* The Queen commented that was *'brilliant news',* Prince Charles jokingly said, *'they've been practicing long enough'* with Prince Harry adding, *'It means I get a sister which I have always wanted.'* The Middletons, too, were overjoyed with Michael and wife Carole declaring that they were, *'absolutely delighted by today's announcement and thrilled at the prospect of a wedding.'*

That afternoon, the couple gave their first joint interview to the cameras, with Kate looking stunning in dress of deep blue, the same colour as the sapphire that winked away on her finger. William revealed he had wanted to give Kate his late mother's ring so that Diana would not miss out on it all. Kate, for her part, appeared relaxed and happy, and it was clear that here was a couple who were very much in love. There was no *'whatever love means'* moment for these two. The next day, the official engagement photos were released, taken by fashion photographer Mario Testino who had been one of Diana's favourite photographers.

The wedding took place at the standard royal wedding time of 11.30am in Westminster Abby on Friday April 29 2011. The day had been declared a public holiday. As with previous Royal Weddings in the capital, London had been royally decked out for the event with Union Jack banners flying from flagpoles in the Mall. On the Wedding Eve, thousands of people camped out on the streets in anticipation of the

Right:

Fiona Cairns stands next to the Royal Wedding cake that she and her team made for Prince William and Catherine Middleton

Left:

Kate Middleton, fiancée of Britain's Prince William, shows off her engagement ring as they pose for photographers during a photocall to mark their engagement

celebrations. Prince William, accompanied by his brother and Best Man, Prince Harry, delighted crowds outside Clarence House by making an impromptu appearance and embarking on a mini walkabout. Kate, meanwhile, arrived at the Goring Hotel in Belgravia where she and her family were to spend the night, having booked out the entire hotel. William later revealed he slept very little that night due to a combination

William & Catherine

ROYAL WEDDING *The Souvenir Album*

William & Catherine

of nerves and the noise of partying crowds on the Mall.

Kate did her own make up on the Big Day — smoky grey eye shadow, kohl eyeliner, rose blush and pink-toned nude lipstick. Hair stylist James Pryce created Kate's demi-chignon with loose waves to give a romantic feel to the *'do'*. As for the eagerly awaited dress. . . Designed by Sarah Burton for Alexander McQueen, Kate's ivory gown featured a satin bodice, which was slightly padded at the hips (signature McQueen) and incorporated floral motifs cut from lace. Burton used traditional Carrickmacross craftsmanship in making the dress, a technique which dates back to the 1800s, to represent *'something old'*. The attention to detail was breath-taking — from the hand-cut Chantilly lace of the sleeves — which drew instant comparisons with Grace Kelly's iconic wedding dress — to the lace applique on the bodice and individual lace roses, thistles, daffodils and shamrocks (to represent England, Scotland, Wales and Northern Ireland) on the ivory silk tulle. The skirt was crafted with white satin arches and pleats to resemble an opening flower. When bridesmaid Pippa Middleton lifted her sister's 2.7 metre train, onlookers caught a glimpse of the lace-trimmed layers of silk tulle that gave the gown its shape. Kate's veil was created at the Royal School of Needlework and crafted with hand-embroidered flowers. Kate's bridal shoes were also designed by Sarah Burton and made of ivory duchesse satin with lace hand-embroidery, again by the Royal School of Needlework. Kate's *'borrowed'* was the diamond and platinum Cartier tiara originally made for the Queen Mother in 1936 and passed to the Queen on her 18th birthday in 1944. Her *'new'*, diamond earrings which were a gift from her parents and inspired by acorns on the family's newly formed coat of arms. Ribbon sewn into the dress represented her *'blue'*. Kate's home-grown British bouquet contained hyacinth flowers (for love), Lily-of-the-valley (for happiness), Mrytle (for love and marriage — and Royal tradition), and Sweet William (for

gallantry — and also her husband).

Kate and her father travelled to the Abbey in a Rolls Royce from the Queen's fleet. At least two million people lined the streets, hoping to get a glimpse of the bride. Meanwhile over 26 million in Britain were watching on TV, tens of millions of viewers worldwide and there were 72 million live streams on Youtube. Kate's maid of honour, her younger sister Pippa, dressed in slinky tube of cream silk also by McQueen, was waiting by the Great West door. She adjusted the train and proceeded to rally the four small bridesmaids, wearing dresses of white and ivory satin and lace, and the two pages wearing uniforms in the style of the Irish Guards from 1820s. The bridal party made their way up the famous blue-carpeted aisle to the anthem *'I Was Glad'* which had been written for the coronation of King Edward VII in 1901. To give the ceremony a country, spring-like feel, an avenue of Maple trees were situated at intervals along the nave. Prince William, sporting the number one uniform of the Irish Guards (to which military tailors Kashket and Partners had added sweat pads under the arms due to the heat of the TV lights in the Abbey), was waiting alongside Prince Harry who was in the uniform of a Captain of the Household Cavalry. When Kate arrived at William's side, he murmured, *'You look lovely, you look beautiful'*.

Much of the service was conducted by the Dean of Westminster while the celebrant was Dr Rowan Williams, the Archbishop of Canterbury. There were no mishaps, although when William tried to slip the wedding ring of Welsh gold onto his bride's finger, he couldn't get it past her knuckle for several seconds. Kate, who, like many brides, lost weight in the run up to the wedding had decided to have the ring made a size smaller for fear it would fall off. The couple chose three hymns for the Service — *'Guide me, O Thou Great Redeemer'*, *'Love Divine All Love Excelling'* and *'Jerusalem'*. James Middleton, Kate's younger brother, read the lesson from the Epistles to the Romans. The National Anthem was sung immediately before the Signing of the Register, after which Kate executed the perfect curtsey before the Queen. *'Kate Middlebum'* as she'd been known at school, was now Her Royal Highness, the Duchess of Cambridge — the Queen having conferred the Dukedom on her grandson that morning. The newly-weds exited the Abbey to the sound of *'Crown Imperial'* by William Walton. On leaving Westminster

William & Catherine

Abbey, to the pealing of bells, they passed through a guard of honour of individually selected men and women from the British services.

A 1902 State Landau took the couple back to Buckingham Palace, cheered all the way by huge crowds thronging the streets. Kate and William were just as thrilled by the occasion as their well-wishers. *'I am so happy,'* Kate was seen saying to her new husband as they entered Horse Guards Parade. Immediately after they arrived, the official portraits were taken by society snapper, Hugh Burnand, who was to later reveal something of the atmosphere in the Palace on that very special day. *'From where I was, and from their point of view, it was two families coming together and that was the feeling, the sense of family and love going between everyone,'* he said. *'They had their own buzz. . .I love them. They are so nice — as individuals and as a pair, and they work so well together.'*

Next up was the balcony scene and the new Duke and Duchess thrilled the crowds below with not one but two kisses, although little bridesmaid, three-year-old Grace van Cutsem, threatened to steal the show by grimacing and covering her ears as the Red Arrows zoomed overhead. Instead of a formal, sit-down wedding breakfast, the Queen hosted a lunchtime reception at the Palace. A team of 21 chefs prepared approximately 10,000 canapes for the 650 lucky guests who had received invitations and were treated to such delicacies as Scottish Smoked Salmon Rose on Beetroot Blini, Miniature Watercress and Asparagus Tart, Poached Asparagus spears with Hollandaise Sauce for dipping, Scottish Langoustines with Lemon Mayonnaise Pressed Confit of Pork Belly with Crayfish and Crackling, and Quails Eggs with Celery Salt. The couple had two wedding cakes. The traditional eight tier fruitcake was decorated with roses, thistles, daffodils, and shamrocks

Left

The Duke and Duchess of Cambridge enter Buckingham Palace by carriage procession following their marriage at Westminster Abbey

Right

Prince William Duke of Cambridge and Catherine Duchess of Cambridge kiss from the balcony at Buckingham Palace

as well as the couple's individual coat of arms, But William also requested a chocolate biscuit cake which he'd loved since childhood. Guests were served Pol Roger NV Brut Réserve Champagne. Prince Charles and Prince William gave speeches but no one gave the newly-weds presents, the couple having asked that well-wishers donate to one of their 26 chosen charities. The amount of money raised was thought to be around the £1,000,000 mark.

At around 3.35pm, Kate and William emerged from the Buckingham Palace gates in a dark blue Aston Martin DB6 MkII, belonging to the Prince of Wales. The car was festooned with red, white and blue streamers tied to the bonnet, rosettes on the windscreen and an *'L'* learner plate on the front. Trailing from the back were heart-shaped balloons and others bearing the initials *'W'* and *'C'* while a yellow rear number plate had been added that read, *'JU5T WED'*. Prince Harry and other friends and family were responsible for the embellishments. A spokesman said, *'It was Prince William's idea to drive his new bride away from the official reception on their first journey as a married couple to his family home.'*

That evening, 300 guests were invited to the evening reception which Prince Charles hosted at Buckingham Palace — the Queen and the Duke of Edinburgh having by this time left for Windsor Castle. Kate wore her second Sarah Burton creation of the day — a strapless white satin evening dress with a circle skirt and diamante embroidered detail around the waist, matched with a white angora bolero cardigan. Her sister Pippa opted for a long emerald green sleeveless dress with a jewelled embellishment on the front and a plunging neckline. William swapped his uniform for black tie. A three-course dinner was enjoyed

of marinated South Uist salmon and Lyme Bay langoustines followed by organic lamb, spring vegetables, asparagus, potatoes and sauce Windsor, finishing with a honey ice-cream, sherry trifle and chocolate parfait medley. Kate's father and Prince Harry made the traditional father-of-the-bride and Best Man's speech, respectively, with Harry reporting to have added, amongst the jokes about William's bald patch and Kate's killer legs, a heartfelt, *'Our mother would be so very proud of you.'*

The massive Throne Room had been transformed into a night club for the party part of the proceedings. *'There was a huge bar in the middle of the room, lots of sofas for everyone to lounge on when they weren't on the dance floor, and a stage for the band,'* said one guest at the scene. William and Kate's first dance was to Elton John's *'Your Song'*, sang by Ellie Goulding who went on to entertain guests with a special set of her tunes. *'Talk about scary,'* she was later to say, *'I was so nervous, my hands were shaking.'* Other songs on the wedding playlist included *'Mr Brightside'* by the Killers, *'Superstition'* by Stevie Wonder, The King of Leon's *'Sex on Fire',* and *'You're The One That I Want'* from the musical Grease which reportedly had Will and Kate mouthing the words to each other as they danced.

The dancing lasted until 3am and then there were, literally, fireworks, in the Palace gardens. Bacon sandwiches were provided for hard-core party animals, which included Prince Harry. After the evening *'do'* had officially come to an end, Harry and pals moved on to Clarence House for the after party. However, the newly-weds were almost certainly tucked up in bed by then. They looked bright eyed and bushy tailed when they emerged the next morning in front of cameras at Buckingham Palace as they took a helicopter to a secret weekend destination. They left for their honeymoon *'proper'* on May 11, having postponed the trip slightly to fit in with William's work as an RAF rescue pilot. The destination? An exclusive, luxurious resort in the Seychelles. Seven years on, the marriage of the Duke and Duchess of Cambridge

is proving to be as joyous as their wedding day.

Meghan Markle describing Prince Harry's proposal of marriage.

'It was so sweet and natural & very romantic . . . he got down on one knee.'

Engaged – November 27 2017
Wedding Day – May 19 2018

Nell Gwyn with King Charles II, Dorothea Jordan and the future King William IV, Prince Rainier and Grace Kelly, Koo Starke and Prince Andrew. . . Meghan Markle is not the first actress ever to have caught the eye of a prince. But as with her fellow American, Grace Kelly, Meghan's relationship with her blue-blooded beau is happily ending in matrimony. On Saturday May 19 2018, in St George's Chapel, Windsor, Prince Henry Charles Albert David will take Miss Rachel Meghan Markle as his lawfully wedded wife.

As has been seen on many occasions within these pages, each Royal Wedding reflects changes in society and the times in which they've taken place. This is especially true of Harry and Meghan's nuptials. Meghan, who was briefly married before, is the not first divorcee to join the House of Windsor but she is the first to marry in a church rather than a register office — as the then Mrs Parker Bowles had to do when she married Prince Charles in 2005. Or indeed overseas like the twice divorced Wallis Simpson when she married the former Edward VIII in 1937. Eighty-one years on from that least celebrated of Royal Weddings, thankfully times have changed. And it is surely something to be doubly celebrated that a Prince who can trace his blood line back to the 7th century Royal House of Wessex and whose great, great, great, great, great grandmother was Queen Victoria is marrying a woman of mixed-race descent whose own great, great, great, great, great grandmother was a slave.

The star of Netflix legal drama *'Suits',* California girl Meghan first met Prince Harry in Toronto in July 2016 where he was launching the 2017 Invictus Games. *'We were introduced actually by a mutual friend,'* Harry revealed during the couple's first sit-down interview with the BBC following their engagement announcement on November 27 2017. Despite Prince Harry's worldwide fame, Meghan revealed in the same interview that she hadn't had any preconceived notions about who he was before they met. *'Because I'm from the States, you don't grow up with the same understanding of the Royal family,'* she explained. *'I didn't know much about him, so the only thing that I asked was, "Well is he nice?" Cause if he wasn't kind, it just didn't seem like it would make sense.'* The two hit it off immediately. *'We met for a drink,'* Meghan recalled, *'and then I think very quickly into that, we said, "Well what are we doing tomorrow? We should meet again".'* The two became romantically involved and by the time Meghan celebrated her 35th birthday on August 4 2016, they were texting every day and she had started following Harry's private Instagram account. Harry, meanwhile, was already falling for the actress. When asked during the engagement interview at what point he had known Meghan was *'the one',* he quickly replied, *'The very first time we met.'*

Throughout late summer and autumn of 2016 Harry visited Meghan in Toronto whenever possible. She also came to London where the couple were spotted on a number of dates. Shortly after news of their romance had broken, social media users noticed that Meghan was wearing a bright beaded bracelet identical to Harry's. In early November 2016, Harry released a statement via the Kensington Palace Twitter account, urging the public to respect Meghan's privacy in the wake of some outlets

making racist and sexist comments about her. *'This is not a game,'* the statement read. *'It is her life and his.'* Later that month, Harry made a secret detour to visit Meghan in Toronto after his 14 day Caribbean tour ended. *'I just couldn't wait to see her,'* he's reported to have said. That December the couple were photographed picking out a Christmas tree at a London market, and also leaving a central London theatre. A source close to the Prince revealed that *'Harry is more serious than he ever has been about a woman before'*. It was mutual with Meghan revealing to a Canadian newspaper that, *'My cup runneth over and I'm the luckiest girl in the world.'*

It is thought that by this time, Meghan had met Harry's father and brother. In September 2016, Meghan was reportedly introduced to Prince Charles at a Balmoral shooting party to celebrate Harry's 32nd birthday. Two months later Harry introduced Meghan to his brother Prince William, with a US source revealing that they *'got on fabulously'*. Then in January Meghan and the Duchess of Cambridge finally met and reportedly hit it off. There was another major milestone in early March 2017, when Meghan was Harry's guest at the wedding of his close friend, Tom *'Skippy'* Inskip, in Jamaica. The couple were snapped cuddling up to one and other, and exchanging looks of love. In May, the Duchess of Cambridge's

Main Image
Meghan at the 70th Annual Golden Globe Awards after party

Above Left:
Prince Harry and Meghan Markle attend a Terrence Higgins Trust World AIDS Day charity fair at Nottingham

Above Right:
Meghan Markle and Prince Harry attend Christmas Day Church service at Church of St Mary Magdalene

sister, Pippa, married James Matthews in Berkshire, and Meghan, wearing a maroon backless gown, attended the evening *'do'* with Harry. In early August, Meghan celebrated her 36th birthday with Harry in London before the couple flew to Botswana to go on safari. Shortly after returning from the three-week African trip, Harry took Meghan to Balmoral to meet his grandmother, the Queen, for the first time. In October, the couple went to Buckingham Palace for tea with the Her Majesty.

Over a year after they'd started dating, Meghan finally talked about the relationship

in a glossy magazine. *'We're two people who are really happy and in love,'* she said. *'We were very quietly dating for about six months before it became news, and I was working during that whole time, and the only thing that changed was people's perception. Nothing about me changed. I'm still the same person that I am, and I've never defined myself by my relationship.'* When Prince Harry hosted the annual Invictus Games in Toronto in September 2017, he arrived hand-in-hand with Meghan — it was their first public appearance as a couple. Harry and Meghan kissed as they watched the closing ceremony. Just two months after this first public appearance, on November 28 the engagement between Harry and Meghan was officially announced. *'His Royal Highness the Prince of Wales is delighted to announce the engagement of Prince Harry to Ms Meghan Markle. The wedding will take place in Spring 2018. Further details about the wedding day will be announced in due course. His Royal Highness and Ms Markle became engaged in London earlier this month. Prince Harry has informed Her Majesty the Queen and other close members of his family. Prince Harry has also sought and received the blessing of Ms Markle's parents. The couple will live in Nottingham Cottage at Kensington Palace.'* A short time later, the happy couple stepped out in the Sunken Gardens at Kensington Palace before waiting cameras and journalists, hand-in-

Left:
Prince Harry and actress Meghan Markle during an official photocall to announce their engagement

hand and looking very much in love. Meghan was stunning in a white woollen belted coat, her custom-made diamond engagement ring sparkling away on her finger. Harry, smartly dressed in a blue suit, had designed the ring himself, using one diamond sourced from Botswana and two smaller stones from the late Princess Diana's collection. The ring was then made by court jewellers Cleave and Company. *'The little diamonds are from my mother's jewellery collection, to make sure that she's with us on this crazy journey together,'* Harry revealed during the BBC interview which followed the photo call. The couple also revealed details of how Harry had proposed. *'It happened a few weeks ago, here at our cottage,'* he said. *'It was just a typical night in for us. . .' 'We were having a cosy night, roasting a chicken'* added Meghan, taking up the story, *'and it was just an amazing surprise — so sweet and natural and very romantic. He got down on one knee — and I could barely let him finish proposing. I was like, "Can I say, yes, now?'.* How had they managed a long-distance relationship? The couple said that they *'never went longer than two weeks without seeing each other'.*

Official engagement photographs followed taken by Polish photographer Alexi Lubomirski, known for his work in the fashion and celebrity worlds, and formally known as His Serene Highness Prince Alexi Lubomirski after inheriting a title from his father. He captured the Prince and his show girl in the grounds of Frogmore House near Windsor in stunning shots that wouldn't have looked out of place in a glossy fashion magazine. Harry and Meghan posed for a formal shot on the steps outside the house — he in a smart navy suit, she in a black and gold embroidered dress by British luxury fashion house Ralph and Russo. There was also a black and white shot of Harry wrapping his fiancé in his winter coat to keep out the cold while she caressed his cheek. The couple then released a third photo from the shoot *'as a way to say thank you'* for all the *'warm and generous'* messages they had received. Lubomirski commented, *'It was an incredible honour to be asked to document this wonderful event, but also a great privilege to be invited to share and be a witness to this young couple's love for one another. I cannot help but smile when I look at the photos that we took of them, such was their happiness together.'*

The wedding day is set for Saturday May 19 2018 — the 482nd anniversary of the day in 1536 when Anne Boleyn, second wife of Henry

VIII and mother of Queen Elizabeth I, was executed on Tower Green for alleged adultery. On a happier note, Meghan and Harry will be marrying at St George's Chapel in Windsor with Kensington Palace issuing the following announcement *'They are grateful to The Queen for granting permission for the use of the Chapel. As with all members of the Royal Family, Windsor is a very special place for Prince Harry and he and Ms. Markle have regularly spent time there over the last year and a half, Prince Harry and Ms. Markle are delighted that the beautiful grounds of Windsor Castle will be where they begin their lives together as a married couple.'* Meghan may be a divorcee but the Church of England has no qualms about her and Harry marrying in church — a prime example of how the institution has changed over the years and moved with the times. *'I am so happy that Prince Harry and Ms. Markle have chosen to make their vows before God,'* said Justin Welby, the Archbishop of Canterbury. *'I wish them many years of love, happiness and fulfillment, and ask that God blesses them throughout their married life together.'*

Before the ceremony, Meghan will be baptised and confirmed into the Church of England. She is also likely to become a British citizen which requires passing an eclectic citizenship test on British life and history, and is famous for tripping up applicants. The wedding day, being a Saturday, has not been declared a public holiday and is fact happening on the same date as a big event in the English football calendar — the FA Cup final. However, as the wedding will take place at 12 noon and the football kick-off will be at 5.30 pm, according to Kensington Palace *'there will be no clash'*. It has even been mooted that Prince William, as President of the Football Association, will be able to attend both events — although that may be tricky if he is to be his brother's Best Man, a role he has thus far denied he is taking on. Bars and pubs nationwide will be staying open later on the evenings of May 18 and 19 in celebration of the wedding. Meghan and Harry are also planning to *'allow members of the public to feel part of the celebrations too'* and are hoping to achieve this by inviting more than 2,000 members of the public into the grounds of Windsor Castle to watch their

Left:

Prince Harry and actress Meghan Markle during an official photocall to announce their engagement

arrival on their wedding day. Twelve hundred of these lucky people will be individuals who *'who have served their communities'* and will be chosen by the Queen's representatives around the UK. The guests will also include 200 people from charities and organisations supported by Harry and Meghan. *'This wedding, like all weddings, will be a moment of fun and joy that will reflect the characters of the Bride and Groom,'* revealed an official announcement. Are these elements of *'fun and joy'* the reason the cake is rumoured to be a banana confection rather than the traditional fruit cake? Of course, they may decide on both. It has also been mooted that the Spice Girls may perform — Meghan was allegedly a big fan as a teenager while Harry reportedly had their poster on his bedroom wall. .

Tradition may suggest the bride's family pay for the wedding expenses, but the Royals will be picking up the tab for Meghan and Harry's celebration. *'As was the case with the wedding of The Duke and Duchess of Cambridge, the Royal family will pay for the core aspects of the wedding, such as the church service, the associated music, flowers, decorations, and the reception afterwards'*, read a statement from Kensington Palace. In another break with tradition, it has been suggested that Meghan may be given away by her mother and it has already been confirmed that she will be making a speech at the reception, thought

Left:
Prince Harry and actress Meghan Markle during an official photocall to announce their engagement

to be because her extremely shy father will not be doing the traditional *'father-of-the-bride'* oration and so she will be speaking instead. Like William and Kate, Harry and Meghan do not wish to receive wedding presents, preferring that friends, family and well-wishers donate anonymously to a charity gift fund.

It is highly likely that the Queen will confer a Dukedom on Harry on May 19 with Meghan becoming a Duchess. The Duke and Duchess of Sussex seems the most likely title — the last Duke of Sussex being Prince Augustus Frederick, the sixth son of King George III, and a favourite uncle of Queen Victoria's, who died in 1843. While Meghan will also hold the rank of princess, she won't be known as Princess Meghan. According to the customs of the British peerage, a woman takes the title of her husband, meaning Meghan will officially become HRH Princess Henry of Wales, but as she's not a British *'blood'* princess, calling her Princess Meghan will be incorrect.

As a former military man, it's a given that Harry will be in uniform on May 19 — but what of Meghan's dress? Fittings have reportedly commenced at Kensington Palace but as with other Royal wedding dresses, top secrecy surrounds Meghan's gown, although it has been rumoured it could be an uber-glamorous creation from Israeli designer, Inbal Dror, after the fashion house revealed they'd been asked to submit designs by Buckingham Palace. Erdem and Alexander McQueen, favoured designers of the Duchess of Cambridge are also thought to be contenders. Whatever the dress. . .

. . .the world can hardly wait for the Big Day!

Eugenie and Jack

You wait ages for a Royal Wedding then two come along at once — or at least that's the way it seems! On January 22 2018, it was announced that Princess Eugenie of York, younger daughter of Prince Andrew and Sarah Ferguson, was officially engaged to her long-time boyfriend, wine merchant Jack Brooksbank — the couple having become unofficially engaged while on holiday in Nicaragua in the New Year.

The groom-to-be presented his beloved with a highly unusual Padparadscha 'pink-stone' sapphire, surrounded by diamonds. The ring is uncannily similar to the one Eugenie's mother, Sarah Ferguson, was given by her ex-husband, when they became engaged back in 1986 — although Fergie's ring was boasted a Burmese ruby at its centre. According to Eugenie, *'Granny is thrilled'*. The wedding, also at St George's Chapel Windsor, will take place on Friday October 12 2018.

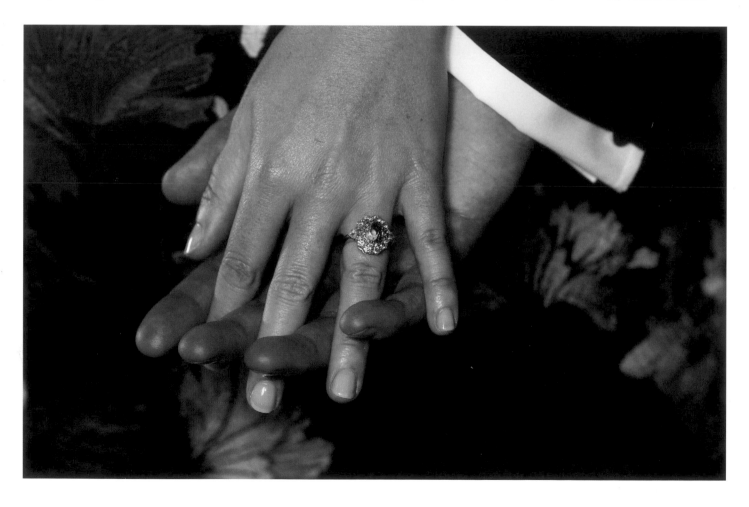